Introduction

What's the big idea?

Domain-Driven Design is all about being explicit about how your object model functions. To this end you need to reason in terms of **hard edges** around the various bits. Defining those bits can be tricky but I hope that with the help of this guide things may be somewhat simpler or, at least, get you moving in a sensible direction.

I will be focusing on practical examples and scenarios that you may run into in your day-to-day modelling and the techniques you may wish to consider in order to implement a pragmatic solution. I will be covering some of the basic concepts of Domain-Driven Design but there is ample literature on the matter so I'll be focusing on where the rubber meets the road. Feel free to skip over the concepts if you are comfortable with in your understanding thereof.

We need to correctly divide up our domain in order to find the correct structure. This will require constant refactoring as we gain a better understanding of the domain. We need to constantly *analyse* our model to break down concepts into simpler building blocks and then *synthesize* them into more meaningful structures. This is something that is an iterative and ongoing exercise.

Remember that at the end of the day we are after a fluid and expressive domain model that will enable us to incorporate changes quicker and focus on the complexity within the domain. Always keep the end user in mind as this is going to be someone who may very well spend their entire working day using a system that you built. There is a great deal of satisfaction to be gained from providing a useful and usable system to one's users.

Target Audience

This guidance is aimed at those software developers who would like additional resources to aid them in their modelling efforts as well as anyone interested in, or using, Domain-Driven Design. However, please keep in mind that this is my *current* opinion on how to tackle the identified issues. You should not substitute it for your own and you do not need to believe everything I say. You may have more experience dealing with a particular problem and, as such, your solution may very well be a better fit. Please do let me know if you have any ideas on improving the guidance. If we get stuck on a particular way of thinking, we'll be just that: stuck.

I will be covering some of the Domain-Driven Design concepts very briefly so if you are already familiar with those then feel free to skip over the relevant sections.

About The Author

Eben Roux has over 20 years of experience in the professional arena as a developer, consultant, and architect within many industries and has provided strategies and solutions that have contributed to the successful implementation of various systems. He believes firmly in the development of quality software that empowers users to get their job done.

His current focus is on domain-driven design implemented within an event-driven architecture based on message-oriented middleware.

> "I'd like to thank my wife Amanda and my two wonderful boys Reynard and Reynier for their love and support in allowing me the time and patience to write this guide in aid of the developer community if only in a small way"

Concepts

Why is Domain-Driven Design so hard?

At first Domain-Driven Design may seem like a daunting experience and you may be wondering about the following:

- Where do I start?
- Is Domain-Driven Design a right fit for my system?
- Would a simple CRUD solution not be simpler?
- Why is it so difficult to identify the concepts?

These are all valid questions and can be widened to include most aspects of design, not just in the computer realm.

An aspect that most people do not consider when it comes to programming in general is that there is quite a bit of creativity involved and creativity is something that is all but impossible to learn. Creativity appears to come to the fore when we are faced with an indeterminate number of possibilities. This leads to one design not necessarily being better or worse than the next but rather just different.

There are different styles of music and each person has a general type of music they prefer. Some prefer many different styles and within a particular genre of music there are also certain musicians or bands that one may prefer over others. Does this mean one genre is better or worse than the next? Most certainly not.

Hard Edges

Is it possible to learn how to be a great musician? One can learn all the basics of music and all the notes, scales, and chords. There is no variance when it comes to this *scientific* or *fixed* part of the music creation process. However, someone may be an excellent singer, pianist, or guitarist but without something original to rise above the rest you can only reproduce existing music.

There are an infinite number of combinations of notes to produce music as there are an infinite number of combinations of letters and words to create stories as there are an infinite number of combinations of paint and colour to produce artwork.

This is also true for any computer system design. There are certain structures (conditionals, loops, classes, etc.) that exist in any computer language and most programmers can pick up those and be proficient in a matter of months. However, there are an infinite number of ways in which we can put these structures together to design a solution. This is the *"difficult"* part.

This is where design patterns and perhaps some practical guidance such as this book can assist by making some concepts a bit more concrete and once we understand these concepts we can reason about a solution in a simpler way.

Object orientation is only one style of programming and if someone is not comfortable with this form of design then it certainly is possible to provide a solution using a different mechanism. Object orientation brings its own kind of magic to software solutions and I'm sure many proponents of other approaches will say the same in respect of their approach. Use what you need and what you are comfortable with. Objects have not failed me yet and are flexible enough to provide solutions for any level of complexity.

It is not that Domain-Driven Design is difficult in-and-of itself but rather that design in general is tricky and it involves a lot of trial-and-error at the best of times. Keep refactoring and try different approaches until you hit something the *feels* right and that expresses the concepts in a fluid way.

Cohesion and Coupling

We have all heard that we need **low coupling** and **high cohesion** when it comes to software design in general. Although we know what this means it can get rather tricky to identify when we are going off-track.

Cohesion

Cohesion relates quite nicely to Robert C. Martin's *Single Responsibility Principle* that forms part of his SOLID principles. We should only place functionality together, typically in a class, when it all belongs together. No definitive list or set of rules will be able to identify all the moving parts that do belong together but if you feel that some parts can be split out without affecting how the class behaves then it may be a candidate for a different class. If you find that you need to re-use a bit of functionality contained in another class, then perhaps that bit of functionality is a candidate to be extracted.

Coupling

Again, Robert C. Martin's *Dependency Inversion Principle* comes into play here. If we can rely on an interface contract as opposed to an actual implementation, then things start going better already. However, this does not mean that all classes have to be an implementation of an interface. Many domain classes require only state based interactions and, as such, an interface would not add any value. An interface is most useful when abstracting behaviour such as one would require in repositories or services.

Another coupling scenario is where relationships are represented in an object model. When it comes to traditional database Entity-Relationship modelling the fact that there are relationships between database entities tends to create a situation where it is too easy to follow the relations as far as they go; and sometimes they could go in circles. This is another area discussed in the guide where we need to create a hard edge around our aggregates.

Behavioural Coupling When one component has to know how another component functions there exists a high degree of behavioural coupling. This should be avoided where possible. It is certainly in order to issue a command to another component and in such scenarios the behavioural coupling cannot be avoided. However, notifications should only be concerned with the behaviour and data related directly to the component doing the notifying. For instance, in a message-based solution we may have an endpoint that can send e-mails. Sending a command to that endpoint requires us to, at the very least, know that the endpoint can actually accept and, ultimately, process the command we are sending. Once the e-mail sender endpoint has completed its processing it should publish an event to notify any endpoint that subscribes to the event. This subscription mechanism should be dealt with by an infrastructure component so that the component doing the notifying need not be concerned with any of the subscribers. In this way we have removed **all** behavioural coupling between the components as the publisher has absolutely no interest in what a subscriber will do with its copy of the event.

Temporal Coupling When I pick up my phone and I place a call and no one answers the call I simply have to remember to call again. This is high temporal coupling since I have to rely on the person on the other end to be available to answer my call at a specific time. On the other hand, when I send someone an e-mail I feel quite comfortable that they will receive it in due course and respond if required. This is low temporal coupling since the e-mail can be sent irrespective of whether the recipient is available or not.

Coherence

I would like to add the concept of coherence into the mix. Whereas cohesion groups code into a class or a method, coherence fits better on a Bounded Context or larger level where we expect the groups of classes to function such that they *pull* in a common direction. A *Sales* Bounded Context has all the classes in the model concerned with getting the sales data and behaviour making sense whereas the *Product* Bound Context is more concerned with product management as a whole.

Business Terminology

It may be worthwhile mentioning that there is a difference between the business terminology and how it maps to the strategic patterns in Domain-Driven Design. There isn't necessarily always a one-to-one mapping between these concepts and we are going to have scenarios where the technical approach has to remain in the technical solution space; the business folks do not *have* to know about these.

Domain

The domain is the total area of focus for our model. Irrespective of the size of the domain you are in all likelihood going to run into a situation where different *parts* of your domain model will belong together. As with most things we will divide and conquer.

Although the following divisions in the domain are given specific names based on how you view them it is largely academic. We shouldn't need to split hairs over this and if you start off grouping the domain into logical units and calling each a *subdomain* then that is absolutely fine for a start.

Core Domain This is the ***main*** part of your domain and carries the most weight. In terms of stock market parlance this falls right in the headline earnings space. It is the *raison d'être* of your domain. This part *has* to work and has to work well and is that part of your system that everything revolves around. If you have a hard time nailing this down it means that you have a rather large core domain. It is what it is.

Generic Subdomain These aid in performing certain tasks in a generic way and the implementation details are not that important to our core domain. Financial accounting and calculation engines could be bought off-the-self and used to perform these functions.

Supporting Subdomain   I think there is often confusion between generic and supporting subdomains. A supporting subdomain isn't something that is generic enough that you would probably *find* anything off-the-shelf available. It would be quite specific to your business requirements but still does not fall into the core of the business.

Technical Terminology

Bounded Contexts

When you consider your business domain as a whole it may be somewhat overwhelming. Not only that, but it may be quite difficult to reason about the various parts given that the behaviour of various classes may seem to change depending on how you interact with them.

It is for this reason that Domain-Driven Design has the concept of a *Bounded Context* where you can group together functionality based on the area they are related to. Typically, you would need a Domain Expert to identify these since we, as developers, hardly ever have in-depth knowledge of any particular domain. As your understanding and knowledge of a particular domain grows you will find that you can refine your design.

Having a Bounded Context at a granularity that is too fine or focused can also lead to problems. You should most definitely not have a single Aggregate Root represent an entire Bounded Context.

Sometimes you may run into a situation where the exact same concept appears in more than one Bounded Context. In most cases this indicates that your Bounded Context is too finely divided. However, keep in mind that it is entirely possible that you need to use the same concept across Bounded Contexts. If this happens you either need to use another Bounded Context to represent that concept or you may need to use a Shared Kernel. It is also entirely possible that you may need to represent an Aggregate Root from an upstream Bounded Context in your downstream Bounded Context. In such as case you will represent it as a Value Object.

Stadium example

To make the concept of a Bounded Context more clear we could take seats in a stadium as an example. A stadium contains seats but the same seat represents different things to different people.

Financial Management   In most scenarios one would have to keep an asset register which is typically owned by the financial folks since they are the *system of record* for any assets.   The finance department would be interested in *data* for an `Asset` such as:

- asset number
- asset type
- date of purchase
- cost
- method of depreciation
- date commissioned
- date decommissioned

They would also be interested in the following *behaviour*:

- Commission()
- Depreciate()
- Decommission()

Maintenance Management   The maintenance department would be interested in *data* for a `MaintenanceItem` such as:

- next maintenance date
- maintenance schedules

The *behaviour* for them would be along the lines of:

- ScheduleMaintenance()

- RegisterMaintenanceSchedule()

Event Management   The event booking folks would be have **data** for a `BookableItem` like this:

- event name
- event date
- seat number(s)

And the relevant **behaviour** would include:

- RegisterEvent()
- SellTicket()

Putting it all together   As we can see, even though a particular seat is a single physical thing in the real world it can mean very different things to different people. This is where a *Bounded Context* comes in handy. You may even find that a similar concept is called something else in each context. You may find that an `Employee` in the *HR* Bounded Context is called a `User` in the *Identity & Access Control* Bounded Context, or an `Author` in the *Collaboration* Bounded Context.

As behaviour is invoked on various objects within each Bounded Context the other Bounded Contexts may need to be informed. To accomplish this one would need some communication mechanism based on an *Event Driven Architecture*. That is, of course, where a service bus, such as Shuttle.Esb, would come in handy.

The *Financial Management* Bounded Context could publish an `AssetRegisteredEvent` and the other Bounded Contexts would subscribe to that event and then determine if they need to register the asset number as an item they are interested in.

When the *Maintenance Management* Bounded Context removes a seat for maintenance it would publish an `ItemRemovedForMaintenanceEvent` that the *Booking Management* Bounded Context would subscribe to in order to exclude the seat as a bookable item for any events until the item is made available again. Any `EventBooking` that has this seat allocated to it may need to kick off some business process to inform the customer about the change and then go about rectifying the situation.

Canonical Models

All this is quite different and in sharp contrast to what many enterprise-level architects refer to as a canonical data model. For our scenario a canonical model would need to include all the data from the various Bounded Contexts. This is quite cumbersome and really does not add any real value. Canonical Models tend to be so all-inclusive that just about everything ends up being optional data and each system interacting with the data would need various validation approaches to ensure that the data is correct.

From a Domain-Driven Design perspective we would want those rules, or *invariants*, as part of our domain code.

Shared Kernel

You may find some concepts in your domain that truly do cross over between Bounded Contexts. These will usually take the form of Value Objects and other infrastructure type classes. You can package these separately and safely share the assembly among your Bounded Contexts.

Ubiquitous Language

The Ubiquitous Language represents an agreed upon set of terms that are specific to a Bounded Context and keeps everyone concerned with the development of the Bounded Context on the same page but it may be just as tricky to define what is regarded as belonging in the Ubiquitous Language.

What I have come across is that we may distill certain concepts into more generic artifacts within the domain model that a Domain Expert may not necessarily be aware of and that there would be no point in even discussing these with the Domain Expert as it may muddy the waters. This is the same reason we should not refer to concepts in terms of database structures or use other technical concepts and terms. We would also exclude all infrastructure components such as `SqlConnection` and the like.

For instance, if a Domain Expert *always* only refers to a **Bank Account** and the client's **Investment Account** we could quite possibly come up with some type of common **Account** structure that accommodates both scenarios. You may be thinking that we could just use inheritance and stick with the original terms but we will be introducing more into our domain model than is required since we would need to implement the associated `Repository` classes also. In the given scenario of only two options it may not seem like a big deal but when we run into tens or hundreds then it becomes almost certain that we need a common implementation.

There may be times when it may be appropriate to discuss the new concept as it may be a business concept that may have been missed, but if you find that it is more of a technical solution to create a more expressive domain then you may want to exclude it from the Ubiquitous Language.

As developers one of our main functions is to identify patterns and distill those into the required *types*. We may be working on an insurance claim system and our Domain Expert may refer to many different claim *types* and mention that each has a set of rules and behaviour that appear specific to that claim type. Whenever we approach this we need to find the lowest common denominator and work from there in order to find the reusable parts. We most certainly do not want to start by creating an Aggregate Root for each available claim that can be registered.

Reachability / Reusability

When we have a bit of code we always need some way to invoke that functionality. We need some way of reaching that code. Here I'm not referring to a user invoking the functionality but rather the *code* sitting behind *that* invocation is what I'm referring to.

We should be aiming for reusability here in an *Open/Closed Principle* sense. Referencing functionality through an assembly or some proxy (over-the-wire) is the go-to method.

The more re-usable the option the more design is involved in order to find the balance between re-usability and business functionality.

Copy & Paste

This is the most simplistic way to invoke functionality that we require. It is also the worst way one could go about doing so. We have a couple of lines of code, or a method, and we simply copy what we need and paste it in its new home. The issues with this are well documented and it leads to a maintenance nightmare.

Referencing Source Code

We could make use of an existing source code file and invoke a method in that file. This is not ideal but a step in the right direction.

Referencing an Assembly

Once we have a cohesive grouping in our functionality we could package that as an assembly and reference the assembly in any subsequent usage scenarios. We can then invoke the relevant functionality by making use of the code exposed by the assembly. Package managers such as *Nuget* are quite useful in such scenarios.

Over The Wire

Another way to get to functionality is by invoking it *over-the-wire*. We can connect to the relevant endpoint using an exposed protocol and then make the required call. This could be anything from a Restful API, a Web Service, RPC, or even using a queue.

Practical Guidance

Bounded Context Granularity

Finding the correct granularity for a Bounded Context is quite important. If you find yourself considering making each Aggregate Root a Bounded Context in and of itself then stop. This is much too fine grained and will end up being *very* confusing. If you have started down this path you are going to have to group your Aggregate Roots into something that is more sensible.

Repositories

Repository A seems to require Repository B

This may be a case of Entity B being part of an Aggregate Root A. Creating an aggregate that contains the entity from Repository B may be the answer. Sometimes things are not as clear-cut as that, though.

Since object orientation facilitates reuse it is quite possible that we have some generic entity that we reuse between aggregates. In the original work by Eric Evans1 on one of the very first pages we have an image that contains the following relationships:

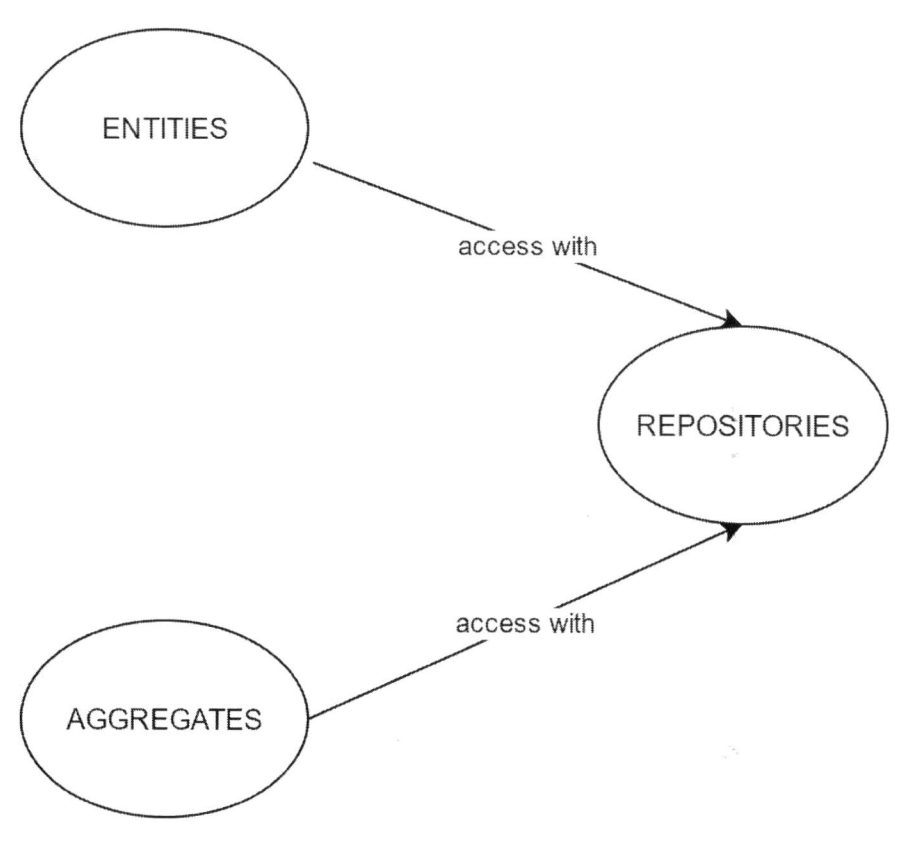

Figure 0.1: *Building Blocks*

Minimal interface

Although the idea behind a repository is that it represents an in-memory collection we should avoid returning list of Aggregate Roots.

To this end we should aim to use the following methods on a repository:

```
public interface IAggregateRootRepository
{
    AggregateRoot Get(Guid id);
    void Save(AggregateRoot instance);

    / not this:
    IEnumerable<AggregateRoot>
        ForSomethingElse(Guid id);
}
```

If you *do* find yourself having a method in your repository that returns a collection of Aggregate Roots you may need to rethink your design. The domain is concerned with commands performed on it and should *not* be used for querying. You also *very rarely* need to alter more than one Aggregate Root within the same operation or transaction.

Repository is responsible for saving Value Objects, even if shared

A repository implementation is responsible for saving any Value Objects that are part of the Aggregate Root. You should never create a repository for a Value Object.

Generic IRepository

There typically should be no need for a generic `IRepository` interface as you are going to need to get to each of your specific interfaces anyway. In some cases, it may be useful when you want to use some decorator functionality such as caching but you still need to consider this carefully. Applying our guidelines around repository interfaces we *could* have something along the lines of this:

```
public interface IRepositoryGet<TId,
    TAggregate>
{
    TAggregate Get(Tid id);
}

public interface IRepositorySave<TAggregate>
{
    void Save(TAggregate instance);
}

public interface IRepository: IRepositoryGet,
    IRepositorySave
{
}
```

If you *do* find that you need to implement some specific decorator functionality it may be worthwhile creating a role-specific interface such as `ICachingRepository` to make the intent clearer.

Aggregates

Aggregate Roots should be one level deep

If you decide to not follow this guideline you will need to carefully consider why you are doing so. To understand why I say this we need to take a look at why one class depends on another in the first place. There are two reasons.

Ownership An example of an *ownership* relationship is a `Customer` having a related collection of `Order` objects. Ownership is only ever between Aggregate Roots. One Aggregate Root may never *contain* or hold a reference to another Aggregate Root. There is nothing wrong in passing one Aggregate Root to another as a transient reference in order for the other Aggregate Root to perform some action. In order to break any direct reference there is typically only an `Id` to the related Aggregate Root or you could make use of a Value Object to represent the relationship.

In the case of an `Order` one would usually store only the `CustomerId`. However, one of the reasons an `Order` can stand alone is that it is an

Aggregate Root and, as such, should one ever delete the associated customer the order would *not* necessarily be deleted. The order has a lifetime of its own. To that end one could create an order without a *real* customer. Think of this in terms of a physical order book. You pick up a pen and write the details into the book along with the items ordered. If you recognize your customer or they give you their *customer number* you could add that as a reference. A new customer that is only going to buy something from you once does not get a customer number and you only record the bare minimum. This is along the same lines as having an account with a clothing store. Some people buy cash and others by on account or use a loyalty card. All the sales can be processed whether or not it is a known customer or a cash sale.

Therefore, we could *denormalize* the customer data into a Value Object that contains an *optional* `CustomerId`. This could be stored as a nullable foreign key in our data store.

Containment   These Entities or Value Objects typically have no reason to exist on their own and you'll find that they also usually represent an *associative entity* in terms of Entity Relationship Modeling:

Hard Edges

Role Aggregate

Role	RolePermission	Permission
Id RoleName	RoleId PermissionId	Id PermissionName

Order Aggregate

Order	OrderItem	Product
Id OrderDate CustomerName	OrderId ProductId Quantity UnitCost	Id Name UnitCost

Figure 0.2: *Associative Entity*

In such a case we'll pick one of the sides as the primary owner. An `OrderItem` is really an *associative entity* for the `Order`/`Product` relationship. Now, if an `Order` should ever be deleted the `OrderItem` associations should also be deleted as it has no reason to exist without the associated `Order`. If the `Role` is ever deleted all the associated `RolePermission` associations should also be deleted. An *associative entity* may also contain any additional data pertaining to the relationship.

Most many-to-many associations will have a stronger affinity with one of the two sides. It may feel as though you need to have the identifier of the *other* Aggregate Root in each. For instance, when we take something like a `Job` and `Board` would be have a `Job` contain a list of `Board` identifiers or a `Board` contain a list of `Job` identifiers. Perhaps the link is so significant that we use a `JobBoard` Value Object or even create it as an Aggregate Root and use the identifiers on one of the ends. Since I'm sure many of us haven't really considered a scenario like this it may require us to give it quite a bit of thought and discuss this with our Domain Expert.

Most of us have come across an `Order` with its `OrderItem` collection. But if you think about it we actually have a many-to-many relationship here between `Order` and `Product`. We typically don't call the relationship `OrderProduct` even though in a purely technical sense we could. We usually *know* that the items are part of an order and make up an *aggregate*. This is the level of comfort we should strive for in our domain modelling. Given enough time and experience we usually get there but it may take a couple of modelling changes to get there. Always aim to break down associations to a one-to-one or one-to-many structure.

Whenever one `ClassA`'s lifetime is dependent on the lifetime of `ClassB` we can safely say that `ClassB` is the Aggregate Root of `ClassA`.

Hard Edges

Example of deep hierarchy   An Aggregate Root is used to represent a consistency boundary. As such it may be necessary to break up a graph that goes too deep. However, you may find situations where the consistency boundaries seem to overlap.

Consider the following structure:

```
1  public class Project
2  {
3      private readonly List<ProjectItem> _items
             = new List<ProjectItem>();
4
5      public Project(string name, decimal
             budgetedCost)
6      {
7          Name = name;
8          BudgetedCost = budgetedCost;
9      }
10
11     public string Name { get; private set; }
12     public decimal BudgetedCost { get; }
13     public bool Started { get; private set; }
14
15     public decimal TotalItemCost()
16     {
17         return _items.Sum(item => item.Cost);
```

```csharp
    }

    public void OnAddItem(ProjectItem item)
    {
        _items.Add(item);
    }

    public void Start()
    {
        var totalItemCost = TotalItemCost();

        if (totalItemCost != BudgetedCost)
        {
            throw new DomainException($"The
                total item cost of
                '{totalItemCost:N}' does not
                equal the project budgeted
                cost of '{BudgetedCost:N}'.");
        }

        Started = true;
    }
}

public class ProjectItem
{
```

```
private readonly List<Task> _tasks = new
    List<Task>();

public ProjectItem(string name, int cost)
{
    Name = name;
    Cost = cost;
}

public string Name { get; private set; }
public int Cost { get; private set; }
public bool IsAllocationComplete { get;
    private set; }

public decimal TotalTaskAllocation()
{
    return _tasks.Sum(task =>
        task.AllocatedPercentage);
}

public void OnAddTask(Task task)
{
    _tasks.Add(task);
}

public void AllocationComplete()
```

```
63         {
64             if (TotalTaskAllocation() != 100)
65             {
66                 throw new DomainException("All 
                       task allocations should add up 
                       to 100%.");
67             }
68
69             IsAllocationComplete = true;
70         }
71     }
72
73     public class Task
74     {
75         public Task(string name, decimal 
                allocatedPercentage)
76         {
77             Name = name;
78             AllocatedPercentage = 
                    allocatedPercentage;
79         }
80
81         public string Name { get; private set; }
82         public decimal AllocatedPercentage { get; 
                private set; }
83     }
```

Hard Edges

In this scenario a `Project` cannot be started if the `BudgetedCost` has not been utilised fully and the `ProjectItem` cannot have its allocation completed until the total cost percentage has not been allocated to tasks. This means that a `Project` can also not be started if all the `ProjectItem` entries do not have their `IsAllocationComplete` set to `true`.

However, this structure is too deep and when we `Get` the `Project` from the `ProjectRepository` we will need to load the `ProjectItem` collection related to the project as well as the `Task` collection for each `ProjectItem`.

Given our guideline that an object graph should be 1 layer deep and how and why objects are related it means that `Project` is the Aggregate Root of `ProjectItem` and that `ProjectItem` is the Aggregate Root of `Task`. This means that `ProjectItem` cannot be contained in `Project` as one Aggregate Root should not hold a reference, other than transient, to another Aggregate Root.

We can break this up using the following structure:

```
1  public class Project
2  {
3      private readonly
           List<ProjectItemAssociation> _items =
```

```
            new List<ProjectItemAssocition>();

    public Project(string name, decimal
        budgetedCost)
    {
        Name = name;
        BudgetedCost = budgetedCost;
    }

    public string Name { get; private set; }
    public decimal BudgetedCost { get; }
    public bool Started { get; private set; }

    public decimal TotalItemCost()
    {
        return _items.Sum(item => item.Cost);
    }

    public void
        OnAddItem(ProjectItemAssocition item)
    {
        _items.Add(item);
    }

    public void Start()
    {
```

```
27          var totalItemCost = TotalItemCost();
28
29          if (totalItemCost != BudgetedCost)
30          {
31              throw new DomainException($"The
                    total item cost of
                    '{totalItemCost:N}' does not
                    equal the project budgeted
                    cost of '{BudgetedCost:N}'.");
32          }
33
34          Started = true;
35      }
36  }
37
38  public class ProjectItemAssocition
39  {
40      public ProjectItemAssocition(string name,
            decimal cost)
41      {
42          Name = name;
43          Cost = cost;
44      }
45
46      public string Name { get; private set; }
47      public decimal Cost { get; private set; }
```

```
48  }
49
50  public class ProjectItem
51  {
52      private readonly List<Task> _tasks = new
            List<Task>();
53
54      public ProjectItem(string name, decimal
            cost)
55      {
56          Name = name;
57          Cost = cost;
58      }
59
60      public string Name { get; private set; }
61      public decimal Cost { get; private set; }
62      public bool IsAllocationComplete { get;
            private set; }
63
64      public decimal TotalTaskAllocation()
65      {
66          return _tasks.Sum(task =>
                task.AllocatedPercentage);
67      }
68
69      public void OnAddTask(Task task)
```

```
70  {
71      _tasks.Add(task);
72  }
73
74  public void AllocationComplete()
75  {
76      if (TotalTaskAllocation() != 100)
77      {
78          throw new DomainException("All
                task allocations should add up
                to 100%.");
79      }
80
81      IsAllocationComplete = true;
82  }
83 }
84
85 public class Task
86 {
87     public Task(string name, decimal
            allocatedPercentage)
88     {
89         Name = name;
90         AllocatedPercentage =
                allocatedPercentage;
91     }
```

```
92
93         public string Name { get; private set; }
94         public decimal AllocatedPercentage { get;
               private set; }
95  }
```

By adding a single layer, we have added a hard edge to our `Project` Aggregate Root.

Aggregate Root A has multiple *owners*

In a situation where you may have some Aggregate Root such as a `FinancialAccount` that may have more than one *owner* the *owner* would need to define the relationship.

```
 1  public FinancialAccount(Guid id, string type)
 2  {
 3      Id = id;
 4      Type = type;
 5  }
 6
 7  public Guid Id { get; private set; }
 8  public string Type { get; private set; }
 9  public decimal Balance { get; private set; }
10
```

```
11  public void Debit(decimal amount)
12  {
13      Balance += amount;
14  }
15
16  public void Credit(decimal amount)
17  {
18      Balance -= amount;
19  }
```

Financial accounts may be related to some `ConsumerAgreement` or by another Aggregate Root such as an `Invoice`:

```
1   public class RelatedFinancialAccount
2   {
3       public Guid Id { get; private set; }
4       public string Description { get; private
            set; }
5
6       public RelatedFinancialAccount(Guid id,
            string description)
7       {
8           Id = id;
9           Description = description;
10      }
11  }
```

```
12
13   public class ConsumerAgreement
14   {
15       public Guid Id { get; private set; }
16       public string CustomerName { get; private
             set; }
17
18       private readonly
             List<RelatedFinancialAccount>
19           _financialAccounts = new
                 List<RelatedFinancialAccount>();
20
21       public ConsumerAgreement(Guid id, string
             customerName)
22       {
23           Id = id;
24           CustomerName = customerName;
25       }
26
27       public void OnAddFinancialAccount(
28           RelatedFinancialAccount
                 financialAccount)
29       {
30           _financialAccounts
31               .Add(financialAccount);
32       }
```

```
33  }
```

The `Invoice` would have a similar structure with its `RelatedFinancialAccount` list of Value Objects.

Keep in mind that no AR may contain an instance *reference* to another Aggregate Root so a `ConsumerAgreement` may not keep a list of `FinancialAccount` instances but rather a list of the related Aggregate Root identities or a list of *Value Objects* representing the related Aggregate Root.

Constructor seems to be getting somewhat long

Keep in mind that an Aggregate Root or Entity should always be *valid*. This does not mean that it should always be *complete*.

You can go as far as having an empty constructor as long as that means the entity is valid. In general, one would need to add that shape to the object that at least, probably, uniquely identifies the object or, at least, something that gives it meaning.

After this you can invoke command or event style methods to populate the entity:

```
public class Customer
{
    public Customer(Guid id, string name)
    {
        Id = id;
        Name = name;
    }

    public Guid Id { get; private set; }
    public string Name { get; private set; }
    public string Address { get; private set;
    }
```

```
12
13      public CustomerMoved Move(string address)
14      {
15          return On(new CustomerMoved
16          {
17              Address = address
18          });
19      }
20
21      public CustomerMoved On(CustomerMoved
            customerMoved)
22      {
23          Address = customerMoved.Address;
24
25          return this;
26      }
27  }
28
29  public class CustomerMoved
30  {
31      public string Address { get; set; }
32  }
```

In order to get your constructor length under control you may need to consider splitting your class into more manageable parts or you could opt to group some of the properties and behaviour into Value

Hard Edges

Objects that are passed into the constructor.

Do not inject anything into aggregates

No dependency such as a service or repository should ever be injected into an aggregate either by way of the constructor or any other form such as the more insidious property injection.

Avoid using repositories/queries in aggregates (double dispatch)

One of the suggested techniques you are likely to encounter is to pass a required service or repository dependency into a method call. Try to avoid that if at all possible.

Calculation Example   Whenever a repository is required the generally accepted approach is to make use of double dispatch. The domain is comprised of aggregates, entities, and value objects in order to encapsulate the behaviour. All those objects should ideally either have the data they require internally when invoking a behaviour or the required data should be passed to it.

If there is no way to determine the data from outside the entity and you absolutely *have* to use double dispatch, then it would be fine.

Hard Edges

However, consider the following example:

```
1  public void Calculate(ICalculationValueQuery
       query)
2  {
3      _internalValue = _internalValue +
           query.GetValue(_idOfValueRequired);
4  }
```

When we have to test the above method we will need to mock the `ICalculationValueQuery` object in order to pass in the value. What the domain is actually interested in is the following:

```
1  public void Calculate(decimal value)
2  {
3      _internalValue = _internalValue + value;
4  }
```

I am certain that when we go back to the ubiquitous language we will probably find that the above behaviour is described along the following lines:

> There are times when we can calculate something on the Widget using a value.

When we truly *do* need to use double dispatch is may be a good idea to facilitate testing using a combination of the above:

```
 1  public void Calculate(ICalculationValueQuery
        query)
 2  {
 3      Calculate(query
 4          .GetValue(_idOfValueRequired)
 5      );
 6  }
 7
 8  public void Calculate(decimal value)
 9  {
10      _internalValue = _internalValue + value;
11  }
```

Discount Example   It may also be that your design can be optimized by making the result of the required call part of the aggregate's state.

We should pay close attention to the ubiquitous language here and especially look out for the word *"when"*:

> There are various mechanisms that we use to determine whether a customer qualifies for discount. *When* the customer does have a discount all qualifying items such as orders and vouchers have to include the discount.

To implement the requirement, we can make use of an event-driven

Hard Edges

architecture using messaging to notify the relevant Bounded Context of the change. Let's assume that we store customer discount information in another aggregate and, therefore, in another database table. The discount, however, is valid only until a given date. We could have something such as this:

```
public class Customer
{
    public Guid Id { get; private set; }

    public Customer(Guid id)
    {
        Id = id;
    }

    public void
        ApplyDiscount(IDiscountVisitor
        visitor, ICustomerDiscountQuery query,
        DateTime date)
    {
        visitor.OnDiscountReceived(
            query.GetDiscount(Id, date));
    }
}
```

The above example is somewhat simplistic since the only `Customer` state we are using is the `Id`. However, it may be that we need to use more of the internal state. As mentioned, an alternative may be to store the discount as a Value Object in the `Customer`:

```
1  public class Order : IDiscountVisitor
2  {
3      public void OnDiscountReceived(decimal
           percentage)
4      {
5      }
6  }
7
8  public class Voucher : IDiscountVisitor
9  {
10     public void OnDiscountReceived(decimal
           percentage)
11     {
12     }
13 }
14
15 public class Customer
16 {
17     public class Discount
18     {
19         private decimal Percentage { get; }
20         private DateTime _expiryDate =
```

```
            DateTime.MinValue;

    public Discount(decimal percentage,
        DateTime expiryDate)
    {
        Percentage = percentage;
        _expiryDate = expiryDate;
    }

    public bool Expired(DateTime date)
    {
        return _expiryDate < date;
    }
}

public Guid Id { get; private set; }

private Discount _discount;

public Customer(Guid id)
{
    Id = id;
}

public void OnDiscountReceived(decimal
    percentage, DateTime expiryDate)
```

```
44      {
45              _discount = new Discount(percentage,
                    expiryDate);
46      }
47
48      public void
            ApplyDiscount(IDiscountVisitor
            visitor, DateTime date)
49      {
50          if (_discount == null ||
                !_discount.Expired(date))
51          {
52              return;
53          }
54
55          visitor.OnDiscountReceived(
56              _discount.Percentage);
57      }
58  }
```

To wire this together a change in the discount status would publish an event that would be processed by the relevant handler to update the discount available to the customer. This would be the most appropriate, and possible only, solution when dealing with distinct and separate Bounded Contexts where the discount is not managed in the customer's Bounded Context.

Avoid using services in aggregates (double dispatch)

As is the case with repositories it may seem as though we need to use double dispatch when using a service. However, when doing so we are coupling on a behavioural level. This should probably be handled by a dedicated domain service.

For example, we may have a somewhat simplified `EMailService`:

```
public class EMailService : IEmailService
{
    public void Send(EMailMessage message)
    {
        new SmtpClient().Send(new
            SmtpMessage(message.Recipient,
            message.Body, message.IsHtml);
    }
}
```

If we need to send an e-mail for an order we could go with the following on the `Order` class:

```
public void SendEMail(IEmailService service)
{
```

Hard Edges

```
3      service.Send(new
           EMailMessage(_contactEMail, "Hello,
           your order has been shipped.", false));
4    }
```

It may not be the best idea to have an order know how to e-mail itself. However, we *could* use the `Order` as a factory for an `EMailMessage`:

```
1  public EMailMessage EMailMessage()
2  {
3      return new EMailMessage(_contactEMail,
           "Hello, your order has been shipped.",
           false);
4  }
```

This may still not be ideal as we may not wish to pull the e-mail generic sub-domain into our core domain. In fact, if we later decide that we could text the customer things would need to be refactored somewhat. We could rather either return the required data or pass in some generic object that we need populated:

```
1  public ContactDetails ContactDetails()
2  {
3      return new ContactDetails(_contactEMail,
           _contactPhone, _deliveryAddress);
4  }
```

```
 5
 6  public void
        ApplyNotification(IOrderNotificationVisitor
        visitor)
 7  {
 8      visitor.EMailAddress = _contactEMail;
 9      visitor.Phone = _contactPhone;
10      visitor.DeliveryAddress =
            _deliveryAddress;
11  }
```

In a more mature environment we may have a dedicated e-mail handling endpoint and an order process management Bounded Context that orchestrates a multiple message exchange that would keep track of when to dispatch a `SendEMailCommand` for the order and then respond to the corresponding `EMailSendEvent` in order to continue the order process.

Apply changes to a single aggregate per transaction

If your data store does not support transactions then this section does not apply.

Aggregates represent a consistency boundary. This does not necessarily equate to a database transaction boundary. However, every attempt should be made to perform changes to only a single aggregate within a database transaction. If you absolutely *have* to change more than one aggregate within a transaction you should give it careful thought.

The reason that this is so important has to do with locking. For higher volume transactions you may run into many more deadlock scenarios when manipulating more than one aggregate in a transaction. Rather attempt to break it into two distinct operations with one leading to the next. This will in all probability require a Process Manager to for the orchestration.

There are definitely going to be times when you *do* need to change more than one aggregate within the same transaction. For instance, let's say we are going to `Debit` one of our `FinancialAccount` aggregates on our `ConsumerAgreement` and `Credit` another. It is quite conceivable that we can use a Process Manager to accomplish this but, on the other hand, we may need to keep it immediately consistent. You will come across the argument that in the real world the two accounts are typically held by different institutions so eventual consistency is implied. However, in our scenario we are not transferring money between two different bank accounts but rather within our domain.

This boils down to how sensitive the data is to consistency. If you can get away with eventual consistency then go with a Process Manager;

else, for immediate consistency, you may need to bend the rules.

Persistence requirements for changes to aggregates

When not making use of event sourcing you may find some instances where you would like to optimize your persistence by not persisting an entire aggregate. You may go as far as having use-case specific methods on your repository: When not making use of event sourcing you may find some instances where you would like to optimize your persistence by not persisting an entire aggregate. You may go as far as having use-case specific methods on your repository:

```
public interface ICustomerRepository
{
    Customer Get(Guid id);
    void Save(Customer customer);
    void Activated(Customer customer);
    void DiscountPercentageReviewed(Customer
        customer);
}
```

In this way the repository may have finer control over the persistence.

An ORM usually tracks changes to objects using a very finely grained mechanism. There is nothing preventing us from sprinkling some hints into our code. When we have an `Order` with 100

Hard Edges

`OrderItem` instances and we call the `.Save(order)` method on our `OrderRepository` it has no choice but to save all those items. When we subsequently change a single order item or add a new one how would our repository save those items? One option is to load all the items from the persistence store and compare them. Another option may be to have some property on our `OrderItem` such as `IsAppended`. When we regard our `OrderItem` as a value object we can replace any **changes** with new items and then when we call the `.Save(order)` method our repository can loop through the order items and save only the appended items. We would need to still remove any items that have been altered. Here we can either keep a list on the order is add an `IsRemoved` onto the `OrderItem`.

This is all still persistence-ignorant since these *hints* are not part of any persistence mechanism but part of our domain code that tracks changes. You will need to make a call on how to deal with these persistence issues.

Always valid classes versus an IsValid() method

Keeping in mind that domain objects should always be valid you may find yourself in a situation where it feels as though you may not have all the data to have your domain object in a valid state.

A typical reaction may be to add an `IsValid()` method. However, you need to ask yourself what that method does. In some instances, it is merely a case of not having a *complete* object. At some stage there is an *expectation* that it is complete and we are tempted to ask the object whether it is so as in the following example:

```
public class Customer
{
    public enum CustomerDiscounLevel
    {
        None,
        Bronze,
        Silver,
        Gold
    }

    public Customer(Guid id, string name)
    {
```

```csharp
            Id = id;
            Name = name;
        }

        public Guid Id { get; private set; }
        public string Name { get; private set; }
        public decimal DiscountPercentage { get; 
            set; }
        public CustomerDiscounLevel DiscountLevel 
            { get; set; }

        public bool IsValid()
        {
            switch (DiscountLevel)
            {
                case CustomerDiscounLevel.Gold:
                {
                    return DiscountPercentage > 
                        15;
                }
                case 
                    CustomerDiscounLevel.Silver:
                {
                    return DiscountPercentage > 
                        10;
                }
```

Hard Edges

```
34                  case
                        CustomerDiscounLevel.Bronze:
35                  {
36                      return DiscountPercentage > 5;
37                  }
38              }
39
40              return true;
41          }
42      }
```

However, it becomes important to know when to ask. Should the repository ask? Also, we may know that the customer isn't valid but we don't know why. Having those setters exposed is also troublesome.

If we attempt to use the **Tell Don't Ask** approach we could tell the object that it is in a certain state and if it isn't the case it can throw and exception. For instance:

```
1  public enum CustomerDiscounLevel
2  {
3      None,
4      Bronze,
5      Silver,
6      Gold
```

```
7   }
8
9   public Customer(Guid id, string name)
10  {
11      Id = id;
12      Name = name;
13  }
14
15  public Guid Id { get; private set; }
16  public string Name { get; private set; }
17  public decimal DiscountPercentage { get;
        private set; }
18  public CustomerDiscounLevel DiscountLevel {
        get; private set; }
19
20  public void Gold(decimal discountPercentage)
21  {
22      if (DiscountPercentage <= 15)
23      {
24          throw new DomainException("A gold
                customer must receive discount of
                more than 15%.");
25      }
26
27      DiscountPercentage = discountPercentage;
28      DiscountLevel = CustomerDiscounLevel.Gold;
```

```
29     }
30
31     public void Silver(decimal discountPercentage)
32     {
33         if (DiscountPercentage <= 10)
34         {
35             throw new DomainException("A silver
                   customer must receive discount of
                   more than 10%.");
36         }
37
38         DiscountPercentage = discountPercentage;
39         DiscountLevel =
               CustomerDiscounLevel.Silver;
40     }
41
42     public void Bronze(decimal discountPercentage)
43     {
44         if (DiscountPercentage <= 5)
45         {
46             throw new DomainException("A bronze
                   customer must receive discount of
                   more than 5%.");
47         }
48
49         DiscountPercentage = discountPercentage;
```

```
50        DiscountLevel =
              CustomerDiscounLevel.Bronze;
51    }
```

In this way we have not only removed the `IsValid()` method but we have also made our domain more expressive.

Don't perform set-based validations in the model

If you have some property that spans an entire set you should leave that up to the infrastructure to enforce. A typical example is a unique constraint such as a unique username or e-mail. These are better handled by infrastructure such as a database index.

You could perform an initial query to check for uniqueness before accepting the command but it is quite possible that a conflict may arise a couple of steps later.

Using Aggregates as factories for other Aggregates

We are all familiar with creating instances of classes:

```
1  // new keyword
2  var paint = new Paint("Blue");
3
```

Hard Edges

```
4  // System.Activator
5  var paint = System.Activator
6      .CreateInstance(typeof(Paint), "Blue");
7
8  // factory
9  var factory = new PaintFactory();
10 var paint = factory.Create("Blue");
11
12 // factory methods
13 var paint = Paint.Create("Blue");
```

I have not seen the factory pattern used very often and it may have something to do with dependencies. In most instances the constructor will suffice. Your mileage may vary.

Creating any object requires input data and the constructor typically requires some basic, mandatory, data that will place the object in some identifiable and usable state. To this end one could use one Aggregate Root as the factory for another:

```
1 var blue = new Paint("Blue");
2 var green = blue.Mix("Yellow");
```

The example above is using a rather simple scenario and in all probability those objects are Value Objects. Also, the fact that the result of the `Mix` operation is another `Paint` object indicates a *closure under the operation* since all the members involved in the operation are of the same set. In most scenarios this will not be the case:

```
1  var cart = new ShoppingCart();
2
3  cart.Add("Socks", 1);
4  cart.Add("Coffee Table", 1);
5  cart.Add("Ping Pong Bat", 2);
6
7  var customer =
       customerRepository.Get("the-customer");
8
9  var order = cart.Order(customer);
10
11 orderRepository.Save(order);
```

Here we create an `Order` from the `ShoppingCart` by providing the `Customer` that the `Order` is for. This technique is only going to work when the Aggregate Root containing the factory method has access to all the Aggregate Roots involved. You may immediately be thinking how that would work since Bounded Contexts should not be referencing each other. The way you'd need to do this is to perform this type of operation using a separate Bounded Context or integration layer that is used to compose the constituent Bounded Contexts or even from a value Object that represents an Aggregate Root from another

Bounded Context.

Aggregate could contain a list with thousands of entries

At times it seems as though your Aggregate Root is going to become too large to load into memory since it contains collections that are huge. The very first thing to remember is that your domain model should *not* be used for querying. We do not want to load an Aggregate Root for the sole purpose of displaying data. If, however, we have access to an Aggregate Root instance that happens to expose the data we require then we could use the instance but chances are that is only going to work in instances where we are working with the specific Aggregate Root anyway. In you *do* go with this option do not be tempted to have your domain code return *any* UI elements.

Next you have to ask yourself whether you truly need to load the entire collection of related objects by keeping in mind that the main purpose of an Aggregate Root is to enforce invariants and consistency. If you require the collection to enforce uniqueness rather use your data store to do that. Your domain is not the best place for set-based operations.

Also keep in mind that if the collection is not necessarily going to be contributing to enforcing any invariants then you do not need to load it. Historical data is probably not going to be required.

Hard Edges

Let's take a hypothetical requirement that a `Customer` may have a maximum of 5 active orders at any one time. Here we can immediately use a collection of `ActiveOrder` Value Objects. We may even keep only an `ActiveOrderCount` on our `Customer` that is kept up-to-date when order statuses are changed.

We may even want to check the invariant on the `Customer`:

```csharp
public class Customer
{
    private readonly List<ActiveOrder> _activeOrders = new List<ActiveOrder>();

    public void AddActiveOrder(ActiveOrder order, int maximumActiveOrderCount)
    {
        if (_activeOrders.Count >= maximumActiveOrderCount)
        {
            throw new DomainException("Cannot add another active order.")
        }

        _activeOrders.Add(order);
    }
```

Hard Edges

```
14  }
```

Structuring Aggregate Roots

Given that an Aggregate Root acts as a self-contained unit one could design the classes to represent that fact. If we take the `Order` / `OrderItem` example a rather *traditional* approach may be to design two disparate classes:

```
1  public class Order
2  {
3      public Guid Id { get; }
4      public string Customer { get; }
5      public DateTime DateRegistered { get; }
6      private List<OrderItem> _items = new
           List<OrderItem>();
7
8      public Order(Guid id, string customer,
           DateTime dateRegistered)
9      {
10         Id = id;
11         Customer = customer;
12         DateRegistered = dateRegistered;
13     }
14
```

```csharp
public Order OnAddItem(OrderItem item)
{
    _items.Add(item);

    return this;
}

public OrderItem GetItem(string product)
{
    var result = _items.Find(item =>
        item.Product.Equals(product));

    if (result == null)
    {
        throw new DomainException($"Could
            not find an item for product
            '{product}' in order with id
            '{Id}'.");
    }

    return result;
}

// mutable approach (A)
public OrderItem AddQuantity(string
    product, int count)
```

```csharp
    {
        GetItem(product).Add(count);
    }

    // immutable approach (B)
    public OrderItem AddQuantity(string
        product, int count)
    {
        var item = GetItem(product);

        _items.Remove(item);

        // perhaps create a new item here
        var result = new OrderItem(product,
            item.Cost, item.Quantity + count)

        OnAddItem(result);

        // or use a factory method (C)
        var result = item.Add(count);

        OnAddItem(result);

        return result;
    }
}
```

```csharp
public class OrderItem
{
    public string Product { get; }
    public decimal Cost { get; }
    public decimal Quantity { get; }

    public OrderItem(string product, decimal
        cost, decimal quantity)
    {
        Product = product;
        Cost = cost;
        Quantity = quantity;
    }

    // mutable approach (A)
    public OrderItem Add(int count)
    {
        quantity += count;

        return this;
    }

    // immutable approach (B) with factory
        method (C)
    public OrderItem Add(int count)
```

Hard Edges

```
84  {
85      return new OrderItem(Product, Cost,
            Quantity + count);
86  }
87  }
```

The above illustrates some techniques that you may be familiar with or have seen before. However, when the *contained* `OrderItem` is structured in this manner it seems somewhat overly exposed.

Another option that makes the association more apparent would be to use nested classes and even a nested interface to allow access to some internals of the `Item` class to only the `Order` class:

```
1  public class Order
2  {
3      public Guid Id { get; }
4      public string Customer { get; }
5      public DateTime DateRegistered { get; }
6
7      private List<Item> _items = new List<Item>();
8
9      public Order(Guid id, string customer,
            DateTime dateRegistered)
10     {
```

```
            Id = id;
            Customer = customer;
            DateRegistered = dateRegistered;
        }

        public Order OnAddItem(Item item)
        {
            _items.Add(item);
        }

        public Item GetItem(string product)
        {
            var result = _items.Find(item =>
                item.Product.Equals(product));

            if (result == null)
            {
                throw new DomainException($"Could
                    not find an item for product
                    '{product}' in order with id
                    '{Id}'.");
            }

            return result;
        }
```

```csharp
// mutable approach (A)
public OrderItem AddQuantity(string
    product, int count)
{
    GetItem(product).Add(count);
}

// immutable approach (B)
public OrderItem AddQuantity(string
    product, int count)
{
    var item = GetItem(product);

    _items.Remove(item);

    // perhaps create a new item here
    var result = new OrderItem(product,
        item.Cost, item.Quantity + count)

    OnAddItem(result);

    // or use a factory method (C)
    var result = item.Add(count);

    OnAddItem(result);
```

```csharp
            return result;
    }

    public class Item : IItem
    {
        public string Product { get; }
        public decimal Cost { get; }
        public decimal Quantity { get; }

        public Item(string product, decimal
            cost, decimal quantity)
        {
            Product = product;
            Cost = cost;
            Quantity = quantity;
        }

        // mutable approach (A)
        public Item IItem.Add(int count)
        {
            quantity += count;

            return this;
        }

        // immutable approach (B) with
```

```
                    factory method (C)
81              Item IItem.Add(int count)
82              {
83                  return new OrderItem(Product,
                        Cost, Quantity + count);
84              }
85          }
86
87          private interface IItem
88          {
89              Item Add(int count);
90          }
91 }
```

In this way all access to the contained class is through the Aggregate Root. This is something we need to strive for since any changes made to the contained objects may invalidate the Aggregate Root. Since Value Objects should be immutable this may be a moot point but in cases where you need to restrict access to methods within a contained object this technique certainly *will* solve that problem.

We can take this a step further and use a `private class` and `public interface` in order to prevent external instance creation. We could *still* use a `private interface`, as above, to prevent external access to internals that are meant only to be accessed by the containing Aggregate Root class:

```
1   public class AggregateRoot
2   {
3       private readonly List<IPublic> _items =
            new List<IPublic>();
4
5       public IEnumerable<IPublic> Items()
6       {
7           return new
                ReadOnlyCollection<IPublic>(_items);
8       }
9
10      private interface IPrivate
11      {
12          IPublic
                AccessibleOnlyByAggregateRoot();
13      }
14
15      public interface IPublic
16      {
17          void SomethingAnyoneCanCall();
18      }
19
20      private class ContainedClass : IPublic,
            IPrivate
21      {
```

Hard Edges

```
22          public ContainedClass()
23          {
24              // can only be instantiated by
                   AggregateRoot
25          }
26
27          public void SomethingAnyoneCanCall()
28          {
29          }
30
31          IPrivate
32              .AccessibleOnlyByAggregateRoot()
33          {
34          }
35      }
36  }
```

Another point to remember when structuring Aggregate Roots is that one Aggregate Root may not reference another Aggregate Root. Now, this does not mean that one Aggregate Root may never hold an instance of another Aggregate Root but rather that we do not want to rely on a deep object graph when retrieving an Aggregate Root.

For instance, if an `Order` and a `Customer` are both Aggregate Roots then the following is most certainly *not* a good idea:

Hard Edges

```
 1  public class Order
 2  {
 3      public Guid Id { get; }
 4      public Customer Customer { get; }
 5
 6      public Order(Guid id, Customer customer)
 7      {
 8          Id = id;
 9          Customer = customer;
10      }
11  }
```

This leads to all sorts of problems. We would not be able to retrieve the order without having a customer object. Where would this customer object come from? Who has the responsibility to retrieve the customer object? Also, when we persist the order, who has the responsibility to persist the customer?

These are the types of problems we solve by ensuring that we have *hard edges* around our Aggregate Roots.

We *may* opt to rather only store some Value Object that contains data that *belongs* to the order in any event. This data should be denormalized into the order:

```
 1  public class Order
 2  {
```

```
 3      public Guid Id { get; }
 4      public CustomerReference
            CustomerReference { get; }
 5
 6      public Order(Guid id, CustomerReference
            customer)
 7      {
 8          Id = id;
 9          Customer = customer;
10      }
11
12      public class CustomerReference
13      {
14          public Guid Id { get; }
15          public string Name { get; }
16
17          public CustomerReference(Guid id,
                string name)
18          {
19              Id = id;
20              Name = name;
21          }
22      }
23  }
```

The relationship is now more clear and we can see that we are dealing with only a reference to a customer. Had we stored only the `CustomerId` that too would suffice but there is nothing preventing us from denormalizing the customer's name into the order.

Just a note on file size: although we should strive toward keeping things small and manageable there is a difference between file size and class and method sizes. For instance, once we opt to include some Value Objects within our Aggregate Root class as nested classes the Aggregate Root class will be bigger. Moving that nested class out may decrease the size of the file but changes little in respect of the design. It may even make it less fluid. One technique you may wish to employ should your file seem rather unwieldly is to use a `partial class` in a separate file for your Aggregate Root and then place the nested class in *that* file.

Invariants

We should be adding all the required invariants into our domain model. Some *rules* may require configurable values and these we can pass in when performing the relevant command. An Aggregate Root cannot do much about factors external to the domain model and you should be cognizant of this fact so that you do not attempt to place every requirement into your domain model. Some invariants may *seem* as though they belong in your Bounded Context but ensure that

Hard Edges

you are not trying to implement an invariant in the wrong Bounded Context.

An example of an external requirement is authorization. I tend to think about a domain model in terms of a physical calculator. It has a keypad with digits, some operators, and a display. If I decide that I want to secure my calculator, I cannot expect my calculator to do so. Anyone gaining access to my calculator can start performing operations provided by the domain model.

Your domain model should be focused on implementing the *business requirements* and not any *infrastructure*, *security*, *performance*, or other requirements. If it can aid in achieving these external requirements, then that is first prize but it should be providing deterministic business functionality in a reliable way.

Any integration layer interacting with the domain has the responsibility to ensure that only authorised actions are permitted.

Invariants involving many Aggregate Roots

An example may be that we cannot create an `Order` for a `Customer` that has a status set to `Inactive`. The first thing to remember is that it is extremely hard to design any software that attempts to prevent a developer from performing a certain task and this should not be your goal. It should be a fluid experience to do the right thing and it should be painful to do the wrong thing. If you can design your software in this way, then any developers making use of your domain model should not be tempted to implement hacks.

To this end it may be near impossible to prevent a developer from creating a new instance of an `Order` even if our invariant states that we may not create an `Order` for a `Customer` with an `Inactive` status. There are some techniques we could employ:

Using the owning Aggregate Root as the factory As mentioned elsewhere this technique is only going to work when both Aggregate Roots are available.

```
public class Customer
{
    // implementation details

    public Order CreateOrder(DateTime orderDate)
    {
        if (_status == CustomerStatus.Inactive)
        {
            throw new DomainException("Cannot create an order for an inactive customer");
```

```
10          }
11
12              return new Order(this.CustomerId,
                    orderDate);
13      }
14 }
```

Enforcing the invariant on a state change The invariant can be enforced using either primitives, an explicit role-based interface, using the owning Aggregate Root, or using a rule container:

```
 1  public class Order
 2  {
 3      // implementation details
 4
 5      public Order(DateTime orderDate)
 6      {
 7          _orderDate = orderDate;
 8      }
 9
10      // option (1): state change using
            primitives
11      public Order Place(Guid customerId,
            CustomerStatus status)
12      {
```

```
            if (status == CustomerStatus.Inactive)
            {
                throw new DomainException("Cannot
                    create an order for an
                    inactive customer");
            }

            _customerId = customerId;
            _orderStatus = OrderStatus.Placed;
        }

        // option (2): explicit role-based
            interface
        public Order Place(IOrderCustomer
            orderCustomer)
        {
            if (orderCustomer.Status ==
                CustomerStatus.Inactive)
            {
                throw new DomainException("Cannot
                    create an order for an
                    inactive customer");
            }

            _customerId =
                orderCustomer.CustomerId;
```

```
                _orderStatus = OrderStatus.Placed;
        }

        // option (3): using the owning Aggregate
            Root
        public Order Place(Customer customer)
        {
            if (customer.Status ==
                CustomerStatus.Inactive)
            {
                throw new DomainException("Cannot
                    create an order for an
                    inactive customer");
            }

            _customerId = customer.Id;
            _orderStatus = OrderStatus.Placed;
        }

        // option (4): using the owning Aggregate
            Root as the rule container
        public Order Place(Customer customer)
        {
            customer.PlaceOrder(order); // <-
                invariant will throw in here
```

Hard Edges

```
51              _customerId = customer.Id;
52              _orderStatus = OrderStatus.Placed;
53      }
54
55      // option (5): using a rule container
56      public Order Place(IOrderInvariants
            invariants)
57      {
58              invariants.PlaceOrder(order); // <-
                invariant will throw in here
59
60              _orderStatus = OrderStatus.Placed;
61      }
62  }
```

Once again we can see that using the owning Aggregate Root would require access to both should they be in separate Bounded Contexts.

We could, of course, decide that our application will enforce this rule but we probably want to get it as close to our domain as possible in order to make it apparent. Security concerns are typically applied in the application layer and will not be a domain concern unless you are actually implementing a security-based Bounded Context.

Hard Edges

External invariants   Some invariants may be "twice-removed" (or more). Your domain proper within your Bounded Context cannot do much about these. Typically, these invariants will apply to a process and you can elevate the enforcement thereof to the process manager itself. The invariants will become part of the process manager Bounded Context related to this Bounded Context. For instance, if we have an `OrderManagement` Bounded Context it will mostly be involved with domain objects within this Bounded Context. However, to implement process managers related to orders we may opt for an `OrderProcessManagement` bounded context that is also aware of interactions with other Bounded Contexts through, say, a messaging infrastructure.

Always valid vs complete

In general Domain-Driven Design practitioners are of the opinion that all domain objects should be valid at all times. However, it is conceivable that we have different stages to the completeness of our entities that change the validity. This is especially true of most objects involved in a process. If we consider our process manager to be a first-class citizen in its owning Bounded Context, then there may be various statuses involved throughout the lifecycle of the process manager.

Each of the statuses may require a different set of data and, as such, we can check the invariants when moving to the next status. Again, we can check the invariants in various ways when we do our call to the `GoToThisStatus()` method.

Apply invariants at the correct level

As can be seen from the examples given thus far we should strive to apply invariants where they are needed. If we consider something like a *rule-engine* things can get a bit hairy. In general, you should really only be using a *rule-engine* on the peripheral edges of your business. You are probably going to be getting the most mileage by using it when integrating with entities outside of your business. It is a kind of generic Anti-Corruption Layer to prevent distorted data from making its way into your business systems. On that note you *may* hear the argument that you can define a rule once and use it in multiple places. This may be so but you have to ask yourself why you would *want* to apply the same rule in multiple places. Most invariants belong in a single place.

Just as we have a *system of record* for data we may think of our invariants in the same way. There is an authoritative bounded context that is concerned with a particular invariant. Anything applying something along the lines of the invariant outside of that space should be there purely for convenience. This is the same for front-end validation. We should *never* trust any provider talking to our domain as necessarily providing 100% valid data. An outside bit of code can act as the gate-keeper regarding *access* to the domain by way of authorization but that is about as far as it goes.

Unique items in collection (e.g. e-mail address)

In general, you should not attempt to perform set-based validations within the domain as domain entities are focused on individual invariants or small, localized, sets of entities or value objects within an Aggregate Root. The most common example of this is some unique constraint such as a `Username` or `EMailAddress` but any key would qualify.

Only throw DomainException in domain

In most cases you should use a well-defined exception class along the lines of `DomainException` or `BusinessException` to identify invariants.

Entities

Using an "Identifier" class

There really should not be any need for anything in the line of an `Identifier` class or a base `Entity` or `AggregateRoot` class. If we *do* make use of a framework of sorts it should be a non-intrusive as possible. It is quite conceivable that we may have different identifiers for different entities depending on their use. Typically, we would use the same key format but we may have to upgrade an existing legacy system iteratively and it could be using auto-incrementing `int` keys whereas we may decide to go with `Guid` keys going forward.

From time-to-time you may run across something like this:

```
public interface IIndentifier<T>
{
    T Key { get; set; }
}
```

The above really does not pay much rent and I suggest foregoing with it altogether. Implement the requisite key directly on your domain object.

Auto-incrementing Ids vs Guids

While on the subject of identifiers we could compare the pros and cons of `int` keys versus `Guid` keys. Some folks are of the opinion that `int` keys are faster than `Guid` keys but I would suggest that this assertion be tested with a good number of records. With the speed of today's data stores I have not found any noticeable difference in performance. Inserting new data may lead to a slight increase in overhead with `Guid` keys as they do take up more space and would lead to more index page splits. But with decent re-indexing strategies in place it all boils down to the low-level read IO.

A *major* disadvantage I find with auto-incrementing keys is that we cannot assign them up-front so it usually requires a read of sorts after and insert to get the newly assigned key. For example, when using Sql Server one could execute the following:

```sql
insert into MyTable
(
    ColumnOne,
    ColumnTwo
)
values
(
    @ColumnOne,
    @ColumnTwo
```

```
10  );
11  select scope_identity()
```

After getting the result from say some `ExecuteScalar` type call we need to assign that `Id` to the entity and/or use it with a dependent object to create the association.

When using a `Guid` we can assign it up-front and use it with any dependent object also. It would only require an insert and no subsequent read. This makes it particularly easy to associate data structures in code without relying on the data store to first generate the relevant identifiers.

Making a role explicit   Although there is typically very little sense in representing an Aggregate Root or Entity in terms of an interface there are instances where interfaces may prove useful. A naive example may be some role such as `IAttributeContainer` that represents some behaviour and/or data requirement on the implementer. In this way we can have a domain object fulfil a specific role.

Value Objects

Value Objects are immutable structures that encapsulate specific data and may contain behaviour. In particular, they are useful when *repre-*

Hard Edges

senting an Aggregate Root or associative entity. When you need to represent *some* Aggregate Roots that belong to an upstream Bounded Context it is possible to duplicate the required data in your own Bounded Context or to obtain the required data by means of an Anti-Corruption Layer. The structures are then represented in an immutable form in the guise of Value Objects in the relevant Bounded Context.

Shared Value Objects

I have run into scenarios where I have the exact same Value Object used by more than one Aggregate Root. You might think this strange but in my calculation engine I have something I call a `Constraint`. A `Constraint` has an `Argument`, a `Name`, and a `Value`. The `Name` represents the type of comparison that I would like to perform such as `Equals`, `From`, `To`, or `NotEqualTo` and can be extended as need be. The `Value` can be any applicable value. As an example I may want to constrain the argument *Age* by applying constraint *From* with a value of *21*.

I now have an Aggregate Root called `Calculation` that can contain a number of `Constraint` Value Objects. My `Formula` Aggregate Root can *also* contain a number of `Constraint` Value Objects. I store my `Constraint` Value Objects in a data store along with an `OwnerName` and an `OwnerId`. In this way I can fetch the appropriate list of `Constraint` Value Objects.

One way to reconstitute the two Aggregate Roots applicable here along with the `Constraint` Value Objects would be to have each Repository build the `Constraint` objects itself. There would be duplication and this is something we do not want. Having a `ConstraintRepository` seems odd as the `Constraint` is neither an Aggregate Root not an Entity. The answer may lie in a `ConstraintFactory` that is used by both the `CalculationRepository` *and* the `FormulaRepository`. In keeping with the guideline that factories are useful in cases where building up the resultant object involves some complexity, we may opt to *not* use a factory if the Value Object is only one or two attributes. But it is up to you. Our `ConstraintFactory` could run off to the data store to fetch and build up the required Value Object or list of objects and return them to the caller.

However, the fact that you even have a shared Value Object may indicate something that you missed in your design. In my case I simplified the structure down to only have a `Formula` and no more `Calculation`. The `Calculation` concept was more of a *classification* that could just as easily be represented by a `Formula` with some fancy footwork. Be on the lookout for this type of thing. Your design may need another look.

Hard Edges

Structure vs Classification

In line with the Shared Value Object thinking it is important to note that we should strive to not include classification in our structural design.

For instance, if we have a `Customer` but our domain experts insist that we have `Gold`, `Silver`, and `Bronze` customers we *may* be tempted to model it as such given the Ubiquitous Language. We could have the following structures:

```
1  public class GoldCustomer
2  {
3  }
4
5  public class SilverCustomer
6  {
7  }
8
9  public class BronzeCustomer
10 {
11 }
```

Instead we could improve this slightly by removing the classification from the type:

```
1  var customer = new Customer(id).AsGold();
```

Hard Edges

```
2
3  // or perhaps
4
5  var customer = new
       Customer(id).As(CustomerType.Gold);
```

However, by making our classification a first-class citizen we could improve our flexibility quite a bit:

```
1  var customer = new Customer(id).As(new
       CustomerType('Gold'));
```

We would need to decide how to design our system in conjunction with our Domain Experts. In any event, tomorrow they may decide to include a `Platinum` customer.

Let's take the example of an electrical plug. Our Domain Expert tells us that we may have a red, a green, and a blue plug. After some discussion we come to the conclusion that these plugs all fit the same wall socket and only the colour differs. That seems pretty much like a classification with very little bearing on rules and/or behaviour. Now another Domain Expert starts talking about a European, an American, and a South African plug. This changes things since they all fit different wall sockets. There may be rules associated with these since they are only going to work in certain countries or with certain socket adapters. There may even be a whole to and fro with regards to rules:

Hard Edges

Expert A: "Each plug can only be sold in the relevant country." Expert B: "What about customers that need to buy a plug for a country they are going to visit?" Expert A: "Fair point." Expert C: "We could show a warning to a user buying from a country where the plug will not fit a wall socket in order that we don't have unnecessary returns."

We could go off and define these various plug *types* as domain objects and add intricate rules but after even more discussion it turns out that we do not only deal with electrical plugs but a variety of products. This changes things even more. We now have need to define rules around some `Product` Aggregate Root. These rules may be rather fluid and we may need to define them in such a manner as to allow them to be added to only certain products. The issue with adding fluid rules into code is that they are not *invariant* and would require changes to the code base every-so-often as, and when, these rules need amending.

It is important to only code true invariants as hard-coded rules. In South Africa we have had a VAT (Value-Added Tax) rate of 14% since its introduction. We would most certainly *not* want to hard code that as an invariant since it *can* change. It *may* never change but the very low probability that it could does exist. On the other hand, we have 15 players in a rugby team. That is an *invariant* as changing the number of players in a team would mean a new sport. If something like that did actually happen it would be something that no-one could foresee and the changes to systems, computerised or otherwise, would be justified.

Is it a Value Object or an Aggregate Root?

There are times when it isn't apparent as to whether an object is an Aggregate Root or a Value Object. The example that typically comes up is that of an `Address`. This is where we need guidance from a Domain Expert. They may not know whether a domain object is an Aggregate Root or not but from talking to a Domain Expert we should be able to determine whether or not we are interested in a specific instance of the object.

When dealing with a physical property of sorts, such as perhaps a deeds office or fixed line phone company would, then an address may very well be an Aggregate Root since a fixed line is probably going to be a semi-permanent feature of an address.

However, a delivery address on an `Order` most probably will not be an Aggregate Root but rather a Value Object.

Factory / Inheritance (Entity / Value Object) vs internal / operation specific interface

A *Factory* is rather useful when we need data from other objects such as repositories when creating a required object. In cases where a specific object contains enough state internally so that it can create our required object we could implement a *Factory Method* within the class while keeping in mind that we do not want to be injecting things like repositories or services into the factory method.

A factory may, at times, even require a dependency injection container to perform its work. In cases such as this it is best to use your *Composition Root* to provide the factory with an instance, preferably through an abstraction, of the DI container. For instance:

```
public class WidgetFactory : IWidgetFactory
{
    private IContainer _container;
    private ISomeRepository _repository

    public WidgetFactory(ISomeRepository
        repository)
    {
        _repository = repository;
    }
```

Hard Edges

```
11      public void Assign(IContainer container)
12      {
13          _container = container;
14      }
15
16      public Widget Create(int id)
17      {
18          var widget =
                _container.GetInstance<Widget>();
19
20          widget.Initialize(id,
                _repository.Data(id));
21
22          return widget;
23      }
24  }
```

Using inheritance in a domain model will have pros and cons. You may wish to use only the generalization and implement the special cases as either a type or by exposing the special cases via an internal interface in the Aggregate Root:

```
1  // using only generalization
2  public class Freight
3  {
4      public Guid Id { get; }
```

```csharp
    public decimal Weight { get; }
    public HazardLevel HazardLevel { get;
        private set; }

    public Freight(Guid id, decimal weight)
    {
        Id = id;
        Weight = weight;
        HazardLevel = HazardLevel.None;
    }

    public void AsHazard(HazardLevel level)
    {
        HazardLevel = level;
    }
}

// using only specialization
public class Freight
{
    public Guid Id { get; }
    public decimal Weight { get; }

    public Freight(Guid id, decimal weight)
    {
        Id = id;
```

```csharp
            Weight = weight;
            HazardLevel = HazardLevel.None;
    }
}

public class HazardousFreight : Freight
{
    public HazardLevel HazardLevel { get;
        private set; }

    public HazardousFreight(Guid id, decimal
        weight, HazardLevel level)
        : base(id, weight)
    {
        HazardLevel = level;
    }
}

// using role-specific interface
public interface IHazardous
{
    HazardLevel HazardLevel { get; }
    void AsHazard(HazardLevel level)
}

public class Freight : IHazardous
```

```csharp
{
    public Guid Id { get; }
    public decimal Weight { get; }
    public HazardLevel HazardLevel { get; 
        private set; }

    public Freight(Guid id, decimal weight, 
        HazardType hazardType)
    {
        Id = id;
        Weight = weight;
        HazardType = hazardType;
        HazardLevel = HazardLevel.None;
    }

    public void AsHazard(HazardLevel level)
    {
        if (HazardType == HazardType.None)
        {
            throw new 
                DomainException($"Freight with 
                id '{Id}' cannot have a hazard 
                level as it is a non-hazardous 
                item.");
        }
```

Hard Edges

```
74            HazardLevel = level;
75        }
76  }
```

Domain Events

Domain Events represent the results of actions performed within your domain.

A Bounded Context may be interested in events that happen within another Bounded Context. The only way that such communication can take place is typically using some form of messaging since the various components are most likely *not* executing within the same process space. There are different approaches that I have come across in order to notify other Bounded Contexts when an event takes place.

Orthogonal Dispatcher

One approach is to make use of some singleton that is relied upon to publish Domain Events:

```
1  public class Member
2  {
3      private Guid _id = Guid.NewGuid();
```

Hard Edges

```csharp
4      private bool _active = false;
5
6      public void Activate()
7      {
8          if (_active)
9          {
10             return;
11         }
12
13         _active = true;
14
15         Dispatcher.Publish(new
               MemberActivated(_id));
16     }
17 }
```

Even though this mechanism does work we are essentially using the anti-pattern form of a singleton and I would suggest avoiding this.

Application Layer Dispatcher

An approach that I would prefer is to make use of a dispatcher on the application layer and then having the domain object *return* an event:

```csharp
1  public class MemberController
```

```csharp
{
    private readonly IDispatcher _dispatcher;
    private readonly IMemberRepository
        _repository;

    public MemberController(IDispatcher
        dispatcher, IMemberRepository
        repository)
    {
        _dispatcher = dispatcher;
        _repository = repository;
    }

    public void Activate(int id)
    {
        var member = _repository.Get(id);

        _dispatcher.Publish(member.Activate());
    }
}

public class Member
{
    private Guid _id = Guid.NewGuid();
    private bool _active = false;

```

```
25          public MemberActivated Activate()
26          {
27              if (_active)
28              {
29                  return null;
30              }
31
32              _active = true;
33
34              return new MemberActivated(_id);
35          }
36      }
```

It may be that more than one event should be returned in which case you may wish to re-look at your design; else return an enumerable or some result object containing the relevant events.

Event Sourcing

Traditionally most of us have been persisting objects using some data store that usually takes the form of a Relational Database Management System (RDBMS) such as Microsoft Sql Server, Oracle, or even MySql. There are also alternatives to storing data in a relational form in order to avoid the impedance mismatch associated with object to relational mapping. Object databases made a brief appearance but never seemed to live up to the promise although I'm sure there are successful implementations. Document databases and *NoSql* data stores appear to be quite the rage and may alleviate some of the pain. However, there are pros and cons to any approach and relational databases have proven to be a rather good general-purpose fit.

Event Sourcing refers to a mechanism where data is not stored in a traditional way. For the most part we have persisted objects and other structures as *records*. These have been a single entry in a table or any other store and we tend to save the entire *entity* in one go. These are database entities and not Domain-Driven Design entities even though they share the name. Even if we only change part of the database entity it is still regarded as *entity-based* interaction. This means that should two users interact with the same *entity* at the same time we need to start dealing with concurrency issues. Well, concurrency issues never go away totally but we can mitigate it by narrowing the surface area. The less overlap our interaction has with that of any other user the better. The chances that two users are going to be calling in to change the address on the same entity are rather slim.

With event sourcing we store the domain events in the same sequence that they happened. An event equates to the result of a *task-based* interaction such as `CustomerMovedEvent`. We then play back the series of events for a given aggregate in order to restore the state of the Aggregate Root. Think about your bank account for a minute. If your bank came to you and said that they will not be storing your transactions but will, after each transaction, only update your balance I'm quite sure that it is not going to be acceptable. We rather like having that list of transactions along with an opening balance for the month. This enables us to track exactly what money was moved and when. Yet for some obscure reason we are quite happy doing that to our data in general. We save the current state and how we got there is totally disregarded. Over the years we have had heuristic mechanisms in the form of *logs* and *audit trails* that indicate how we got to the state that we are in but these are quite often lacking in some form unless particular attention is brought to them.

Event Sourcing brings the auditing front-and-center in that it the source of truth. It is our list of *transactions*. In most cases folks immediately have some concerns and questions:

- Isn't this going to get rather slow over time?
- How do I query this list of events?
- Where are my foreign keys and unique constraints?

These are all valid questions but the challenges are most certainly not insurmountable.

Dealing with a large number of events   Back to your bank account. You do not receive a statement every month containing all your transactions from the day your account became active. Instead each month starts with an opening balance. That is a heuristic called a *snapshot*. What would happen if the bank happened to lose all opening/closing balances for your account? Nothing. They would simply "rebuild" them from the existing transactions. This is exactly how you could approach your event store. You could create snapshots containing a summary of your entire Aggregate Root whenever required. To rebuild your Aggregate Root, you would load the last snapshot and apply any new events after that point. Snapshots work along the lines of the *momento pattern*.

Some event stores save only a single snapshot and rebuild from there. if you can use an event store that includes the snapshots as part of the event stream you may gain some benefit in that you could store various snapshots that make sense to your domain and rebuild from that particular snapshot.

Querying the event store An event store shares some similarity to a messaging queue and in such an environment you would not query a queue and there would be little sense in doing so. Although there would probably be more sense in querying an event store it is also something that you should try to avoid. Even if you could you would need some form of tooling and it would probably be closer to an operational task than an everyday run-of-the-mill function in your application. The events are serialized objects that contain the outcome of an action and as such need to be transformed into something more readable.

This is where **Event Projection** comes to the fore. Event Projection can be thought of as a cursor running over each and every event in your event store. There are some mechanisms to perhaps skip over certain event types but for the most part we would be scanning over the entire set. The job of a projection is to take an event and denormalize the data into a *read model* that can be easily queried. This would then be used by your front-end or reporting Bounded Context to access the required data.

Each individual projection runs through each event in sequence but different projections can be run in parallel. For instance, we may have a *Customer* projection and a *Product* projection. Should we discover some error in our projection code we could quite easily create a new projection with the fix and run through it. Once it has caught up to the head of the event store we could disable the erroneous projection and enable our new projection.

Events should be clustered around the Aggregate Root identifier as we need to reconstitute an Aggregate Root from all the events related to that identifier. Projections, on the other hand, run using some global sequence number that runs across *all* the events in the event store.

Hard Edges

Unique Constraints and Foreign Keys   Since there is no way to tell whether a particular event contains unique data without running through the entire event store we need some other place to store any unique values. Any indexing mechanism will do but it has to be used in isolation and may not even necessarily be part of the event store; although some would certainly provide such a mechanism as a convenience.

Querying possibilities by way of a cricket/baseball example   In the sport "cricket" the scoring is rather detailed. So-much-so that it actually closely resembles event sourcing. Now, it is most certainly possible to store only the outcome of the game with a summary of the wickets taken, extras, balls bowled, etc. However, the scorers typically record the events around each and every ball bowled. This allows one to come up with totally new queries such as "how many times did a bowler take three wickets in the second over of a test match on the second day?". In this same way we may be able to answer a business query such as "how many customers moved more than once in the last five years?" for our customer management system when we use event sourcing. Again, there are perhaps other ways to get to the data for such a query in a more traditional way, *if* we were storing some semblance of the data somewhere. But with event sourcing we could create a new projection and run it over the history of our event store at any time in the future.

Another bat-and-ball game that this could apply to is "baseball". If the data concerned with every pitch is stored, we could ask a brand new query such as "how many times have the bases been filled in the fifth inning on the fifth pitch?". Without event sourcing such a query would probably be impossible to answer.

Messaging

Any time we deal with domain events and we need inter-process communication we are going to require some messaging infrastructure. It may be possible to roll your own that targets a specific queuing mechanism. This is fine but you may want to consider using a service bus of sorts. There are many distributed service bus options in the .Net space such as Shuttle.Esb, MassTransit, NServiceBus, and Rebus (and I'm sure there may be more). These mechanisms buy you quite a bit out-of-the-box. At the most basic level they provide an abstraction over a queue by placing a message onto a queue and then having some process that reads that message out of the queue and passed it to some message handler that processes it.

It is important to note that messages are plain data transfer objects and exhibit no behaviour. If you ever *do* find that you would like to add some auxiliary method to the message, I'd recommend an extension method since some methods may interfere with your serialization implementation.

Hard Edges

In this way you may send a *command* telling your domain to do something:

```
public class RegisterMemberCommand
{
    public string Name { get; set; }
}
```

This message should be routed by your service bus from the originator, say a web-api, to the relevant processing endpoint where the member will be registered using your domain model. That endpoint may then publish that event:

```
public class MemberRegisteredEvent
{
    public Guid Id { get; set; }
    public string Name { get; set; }
}
```

Any other Bounded Context that is interested in that event would subscribe to that message type and receive a copy, via the service bus, of that event. This would allow the recipient to perform some relevant processing.

Hard Edges

System Events vs Domain Events

There are some folks that are of the opinion that we do not need a service bus as an event store can serve as our publishing source. I agree 100% with the event store providing the *domain events* but I would not agree that it replaces the need for a service bus fully. Of course I have a dog in the fight so I am quite biased. However, as events go into the event store each may have a `DatePublished` stored along with the event in the relevant store. The `DatePublished` is not part of the event but rather forms part of the infrastructure. The `DatePublished` would start out as a `NULL`. There would be some processor that picks up any events that have not yet been published and then publishes them using the service bus. The relevant event entry then has the `DatePublished` set.

Integrating Bounded Contexts

When we decouple our Bounded Contexts, and other software components, to the desired level it may require some additional thinking in terms of how we integrate them again. Looking at that sentence it seems quite odd to pull things apart and then having to think about how to put them back together. At the end of the day it boils down the properly identifying cohesive units that perform individual bits of functionality well. These should be easier to test since we should aim to keep the number of interactions low. To illustrate keeping interactions low I can use an example I have seen that deals with traditional dice. If we throw a single die we can have 6 outcomes. If we pick up two dice we can have six to the power of two options, so 6 x 6 = 36. Now if we had to pick up three dice we would have 6 x 6 x 6 which would leave us with 216 options. As we can see, this can get out of hand pretty quickly. What if we could split these into individual interactions? Then we would have 3 x 6 options which would be 18. Quite a bit easier to work with.

When integrating Bounded Contexts, we are going to either require data from another Bounded Context or request another Bounded Context to perform some action. Defining those edges clearly and keeping them as far apart as possible is going to go a long way in reasoning about the interactions.

Querying our Read Model

The query side of our domain is along the lines of old-school OLAP (Online Analytical Processing) albeit less warehouse-, or, analytically-focused but most definitely geared towards being optimized for reading/querying of data.

In order to query our read model, we would need to expose it somehow. At the very least we need an API to do so. As somewhat of a

Hard Edges

convention I tend to suffix my queries using `Query`. If you find yourself contemplating how to expose your Aggregate Roots via a repository you should immediately try to think in terms of a query layer. There are going to be very few instance where your repository should go beyond a `Get(id)` and `Save(object)` method as a repository would be dealing mostly with fully constituted Aggregate Roots.

Let's assume that we feel the need to add a method to our repository to find the most recent orders for a customer. Initially we decide we need the following on our repository:

```
1  public interface IOrderRepository
2  {
3      IEnumerable<Order> MostRecent(Guid
           customerId, int count);
4  }
```

We are now going to create possibly `count` number of `Order` instances. We decide that we have no need for the `OrderItem` collection so we need some way to exclude those. Now our domain is going to somewhat involved in our data access fetching strategies. As soon as we see lazy-loading you know that you are querying your domain model. This is something that should be avoided as it creates far more issues than it solves.

A more natural and focused approach would be to create a dedicated query layer:

```
IEnumerble<DataRow> MostRecent(Guid 
    customerId, int count);
```

However, if we decide that we do not wish to retrieve raw data out of something like a `DataRow` we may opt for a specific data transfer object (DTO). One option may be to create a very specifically named DTO such as `MostRecentOrder`. Even so, I tend to create a query-specific namespace for these objects. This would allow one to use the same name for the object where appropriate:

```
namespace Project.Query
{
    public class Order
    {
        public DateTime DateRegistered { get; set; }
        public decimal Total { get; set; }
        public string CustomerName { get; set; }
    }
}
```

The interface/implementation would then change to the following:

```
1    IEnumerble<Query.Order> MostRecent(Guid
         customerId, int count);
```

One could use very simple convention-based mapping to populate the DTO as it should be a plain data container with puclic getters and setters.

If need be these same objects may be exposed via a Web/Rest API. One would typically issue a `GET` request to obtain data. There may be times where it seems as though a `POST` may be more appropriate and, if so, do not hesitate to use that. You may even need a combination. For instance, you may wish issue a `POST` that effectively requests processing via some `command` (see next section). As an example we may request that a quote or report be generated. Once complete some notification mechanism makes its way to the front-end where we then issue a `GET` request to return the result using, most probably, some unique identifier. This may work equally well to perform saved searches where we issue a `POST` containing search criteria. Once the search has completed the front-end is notified that the search is complete and the requested data is returned. This mechanism should only be used in specific scenarios where the search is required to be saved and may be computationally expensive to perform. Typically, a simple request/response style `GET` request should suffice.

Hard Edges

Sending Commands to our Domain Model

The domain model is more aligned to old-school OLTP (Online Transaction Processing). Our Aggregate Roots would be where the innermost execution of commands would take place. You would expose the Aggregate Root method via an API of the Bounded Context and this may include domain services. A Web/Rest API could also be used where you could issue a `POST`, `PUT`, or `DELETE` verb to perform the relevant processing. Your web-based endpoint may actually issue a service bus command or place some request on a queue using direct access and then return an HTTP 200 status code to indicate that the request has been accepted. Any asynchronous processing with greatly improve the scalability of your system.

Value Objects in downstream Bounded Contexts

When we require data from an Aggregate Root in an upstream Bounded Context it may make sense to store a copy of a subset of the data related to that upstream Aggregate Root. In some instance that data may manifest as an Entity or Aggregate Root in-and-of-itself in *our* Bounded Context. For instance, the *Finance* Bounded Context may contain a list of assets and when a new asset is added the *Maintenance* Bounded Context is notified via an event. However, we store our `MaintenanceItem` as an Aggregate Root since we are able

Hard Edges

create arbitrary `MaintenanceItem` entries ourselves. When we *do* create a new `MaintenanceItem` Aggregate Root from a new asset we would add some indicator in order to be aware of that link should we receive other events from the *Finance*, or other, Bounded Context that requires us to take some action on our `MaintenanceItem` relate to a specific asset.

The same goes for a Value Object. We will not be making changes directly to our list of Value Objects in the sense of an Entity but we could and probably *should* make changes when we receive notifications from the *Assets* Bounded Context that relates to the relevant Value Object.

Messaging

When using a messaging infrastructure, I would suggest having an endpoint that deals with process management and another that deals with commands:

Hard Edges

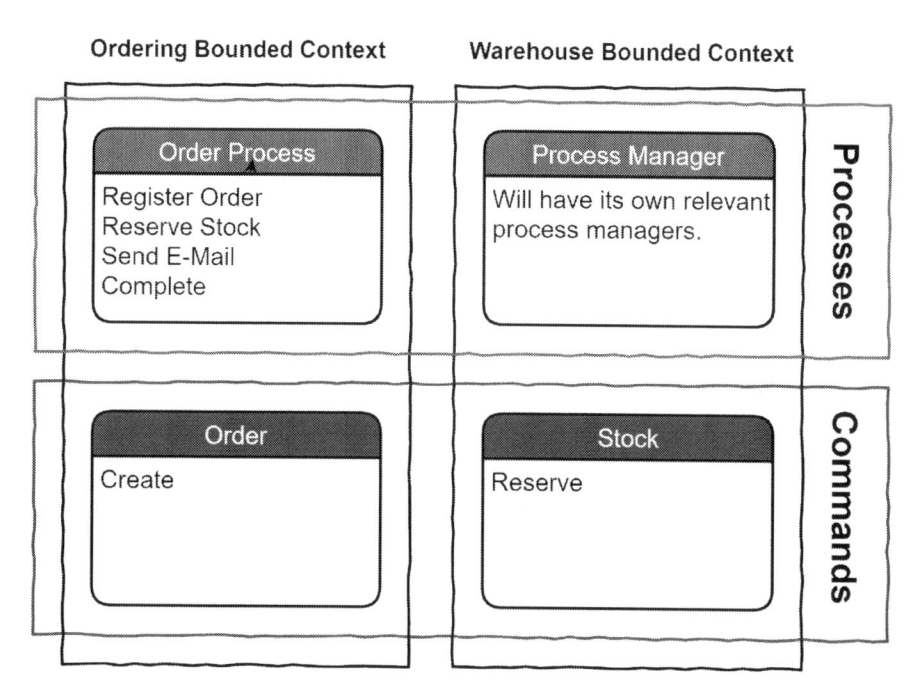

Figure 0.3: *Bounded Context Interaction*

The *command* layer typically would not be responding to any events but only commands and then, once completed, would publish an event that would be subscribed to by the relevant process management endpoints.

Anti-Corruption Layer

Domain objects should steer clear of requesting data or calling out of the domain to external infrastructure components such as third-party interfaces. Instead, rather make use of an Anti-Corruption Layer to provide the required objects to the domain. These ACLs will typically provide Value Objects that may be consumed by your domain code.

Project Structure / Modules

Project structure will be highly dependent on your deployment and infrastructure. There is not going to be a one-size-fits-all structure. I tend to take the approach of keeping things as close together as possible and only split out to separate assemblies when required. One needs to pay particular attention to coupling between classes when doing so as to minimize any pain when moving bits out to another assembly. I find project folders particularly useful in such cases and you may opt to namespace your classes based on those folder structures.

I tend to create a solution for each Bounded Context. Assuming we have an accounting Bounded Context we may have something along these lines:

```
1  Shuttle.Accounting.sln
```

```
2      Shuttle.Accounting.csproj
3          // contains domain model
4          DataAccess
5              // folder containing repository
                  implementation (good candidate
                  for own assembly)
6          Query
7              // contains read models
8          DomainServices
9              // contains domain services
10     Shuttle.Accounting.Server.csproj
11         // service bus integration lay
12     Shuttle.Accounting.Projection.csproj
13         // event source projection processing
14     Shuttle.Accounting.Processes.csproj
15         // process management
16     Shuttle.Accounting.WebApi.csproj
17         // web-api that would typically
                provide query result or issue
                commands to the server project
18     Shuttle.Accounting.Site.csproj
19         // using your favourite
                JavaScript.MV* library such as
                CanJS
20     Shuttle.Accounting.Shell
21         // perhaps using WinForms / WPF
```

Microservices & Context Maps

As is the norm in the development community, there is no shortage of new techniques and their accompanying names. It is also quite often the case that many of these concepts are not really new and it may at times be quite difficult to nail down a proper definition.

Micoroservices is one of those tricky things that *feel* as though it should be profound but I doubt whether it really is. When it comes to software re-use we are going to be dealing with deployment units. As stated elsewhere this ranges from copying code or a file, linking to a file, or even using an assembly in a separate package. Microservices are more closely related to Service Oriented Architecture (SOA) in that they provide a service of some kind. Even so, any SOA is going to be something that, on a logical level, provides loosely-coupled services. It seems as though Microservices aim to have more finely-grained services than one would typically find in a SOA where there seems to have been a higher regard for coarse-grained interfaces.

I have seen a very good presentation by Eric Evans about how Bounded Contexts map quite nicely into this style. Now, a Bounded Context may not be "micro" by any stretch of the imagination but a single Bounded Context most certainly should be a deployment unit

Hard Edges

if one takes into consideration that one could regard anything from the front-end, and reporting, all the way to process management as Bounded Contexts this certainly would hold true. Of course if one were to take something like reporting it would also be vertically sliced along various Bounded Contexts. For example, reporting for Accounting, Product, Orders, etc.

I tend to take more of a separation-of-concerns view to these things rather that to try and name them using the latest term. If any term does assist in expressing the concept, then that is first prize.

It may be that the idea behind microservices fit more closely to generic subdomains where there is a very acute focus on re-use given their generic nature. If we can identify such generic parts within our domain, it would greatly improve re-use and fit in nicely with the microservices ideal. However, it takes a great deal of understanding of a domain (or several) in order to identify these moving bits.

Command-Query Responsibility Segregation (CQRS)

Many people see CQRS and immediately assume that it implies, or is the same thing as, Event Sourcing. If you are familiar with the difference you may wish to skip this section.

CQRS has its roots in the concept of Command-Query Separation suggested by Bertrand Meyer. The basic concept to understand when

Hard Edges

it comes to CQRS is that you separate your commands/actions from your queries/reads. This sounds like common sense and we tend to believe that we are already doing so. However, if you ever find yourself querying your domain model then you are not practicing CQRS.

There are probably going to be instances where you find that all the information you require can be exposed by your Aggregate Root and in such situations it is probably okay to do so. These situations are typically limited to those where you require data from a single Aggregate Root. Anything related to display or lists usually would require a query layer. This is where CQRS shines. You may even opt to denormalize some data in your read store.

Many folks also believe that CQRS implies *eventual consistency* but this is not necessarily the case. There are a number of ways you can approach CQRS.

- Read from the same table in the same data store.
- Read from another table in the same data store.
- Read from a dedicated data store optimized for querying.

You may also decide to have certain queryable data 100% consistent whilst others may be eventually consistent. If you can get away with eventual consistency the scalability of your system will probably benefit. However, there are some scenarios where we are going to need 100% consistency between the query data and the transactional data.

Hard Edges

An example is a bank balance. It is, of course, totally possible to use eventual consistency and may very well be acceptable but it will depend on the use case. Assume that two people have an ATM card for the same account and both decide to withdraw the last $100 from the account using different ATM machines at, as luck would have it, the *same* time. The command to withdraw is sent to the server and the balance is checked before issuing the money. If both transactions are successful the account will be overdrawn and, in our case, this is not permitted. There may be arguments either way but you are going to run into these situations and they need to be dealt with on a case-by-case basis.

That being said, you should make every effort to explain to your Domain Expert that not every action in the system requires 100% consistency. In real life we have many examples where we are waiting for something to happen asynchronously. For some odd reason many people have an expectation that a computerised system has infinite resources and that just isn't true. When applying for a passport, for instance, you fill in your application form and go to the submission counter. Your form is validated and once found to be complete you are expected to pay some fee. Your request message (application) is then sent off for some processing and you take with you some document as proof of your application and payment and go home. Very few people end up standing at the counter waiting for their passport to come back immediately. Sometime later you are notified by e-mail or text message that your passport is ready for collection. This is an eventually consistent and asynchronous process. We do these things all the time and we need to get our Domain Experts to get on board with this kind of thinking.

Query namespace for query objects

There are times when you need a dedicated read model. These classes are also referred to as Data Transfer Objects. A separate query layer is recommended and if you follow some of this guidance you may end up with a read model that feels as though it should have the same name as your Aggregate Root. Since your read model is closely related to querying you may decide to keep it in the same assembly where your repository infrastructure components live. You may opt for a separate assembly containing but if they do happen to be in one assembly and you find conflicts with naming an option is to namespace the read models.

```
namespace Company.BoundedContext.DataAccess.Query
{
    public class Order
    {
        public string OrderNumber { get; set;
        }
```

Hard Edges

```
6            public DateTime DateRegistered { get;
                set; }
7            public string CustomerName { get;
                set;}
8            public decimal Total { get; set; }
9        }
10   }
```

Queries that seem to require domain operations to be duplicated

If you find that in order to fulfil a query you need to apply domain logic it may be an indication that you should not be querying in the first place. You most certainly should get the data back to your user but probably in a more round-about way. For instance, assume that your user would like a sales forecast for a given period. This may require some serious *processing* and domain logic. In this case you should design the system such that the user can issue a *request* for the forecast and, once it has been completed, the system will notify the user that the report/forecast has been completed and that the data can be viewed. This frees up the server to schedule the work and the user can continue with other tasks in the meantime.

Such a mechanism may be appropriate for general reporting even when no additional processing is required. If we run into a situation where 200 users decide that they need to view their report at the same time and we process all reporting requests immediately then our reporting and database servers are definitely going to be taking strain. However, if a request for a report is issued and placed on a queue using a service bus or some custom-rolled queuing we could have our reporting server endpoint handle, say, a maximum of 5 concurrent report requests. This places less strain on the computing resources and improves the user experience for all users.

Application and Domain Services

A *domain service* should be used when interacting with multiple domain objects or having behaviour that does not seem to fit on any single class.

An *application service* is typically a coarse-grained service that wraps various operations on the domain model. It should not contain any business logic. To this end I do not find too much use in these and would only use an application service if the need arises. There are folks that reckon that the effort is so small that one may as well add these from the get-go but if I don't need it immediately I'd spend that same small effort if-and-when I do.

Domain and application services may be implemented to perform a single function, such as `Execute` à la the *Command Pattern*, or it may be more coarse-grained where there would be a method per function, such as `Take()`, `Confirm()`, `Dispatch()`. This is more of a preference than having any particular impact on system design; although having to only perform a single function is going to lead to smaller classes and will aid in achieving the *Single Responsibility Principle*.

In order to avoid using namespaces to identify domain and application services one could use a suffix of `Service` for the domain and `Task` for the application service.

Note on processes

In many cases where we are using a domain or application service it may be to complete some sequential process. You may very well find yourself interacting with multiple Aggregate Roots in a single transaction. It is possible to break up such a process into its distinct steps and implement a message-based process manager. The process manager will become a first-class citizen in your domain and keep track of the process. This may seem like a bit more work but there are going to be pros and cons to this approach and given your project constraints and requirements you will have to make a pragmatic call on this.

Deleting

For the most part we should aim to not ever delete any data in the transactional data. If there is a need to delete any data in order to replace it then that operation should always be in a database transaction. If your data store does not support transactions, then go with a journal approach where you write first and *then* delete. If you are using Referential Integrity, it typically only needs to exist on your transactional store.

Your read store is another matter. No Referential Integrity is necessarily required although you may wish to configure cascading deletes.

If you are using only a single data store for both transactional and read operations, then you would go with the guidelines around the transactional data store.

Techniques, Technologies, and Questions

ORMs

When making use of a relational database to persist your domain objects you may be considering the use of an Object-Relational Mapper such as NHibernate or Entity Framework. Even though you are *always* going to be performing object-relational mapping in the sense of the **Data Mapper** pattern you may find that adding another layer in the form of ORM tooling may add even more mapping to the mix.

You may find that there is a sufficient disconnect between your domain structure and your database structure that you are going to need database-specific versions of the entities. You may also find that your tooling requires you to structure certain parts of your domain model in a specific way that may not be what you want.

I am no proponent of ORMs and would suggest that you use Ado.Net directly for your data mapping.

Why can an Address sometimes be an Aggregate Root and other times a Value Object?

Every-so-often the question of whether an address is an Aggregate Root or a Value Object seems to pop up somewhere. You *may* have folks argue either way and present their case but for the most part it is going to depend on the use of the `Address`. This is why there may be confusion.

Any business that has infrastructure with a termination point at a physical address may regard an `Address` as an Aggregate Root. Examples may be fixed telephone line operators, fibre providers, or security companies that place a radio on your premises.

On the other hand, our online shop may require an address in order to deliver the box of electrical plugs you ordered. In this case they are not interested in the lifetime of the address and the `Address` is a Value Object.

It may be that you have *both* scenarios in your domain. In such a case you may wish to name them appropriately. For example, our Aggregate Root may be `TerminationAddress` and our Value Object `PhysicalAddress`.

Making the system do a lot of work vs. making the user do a lot of work

In many situations it takes a lot of effort to make things simple for a user. Typically, various individual functions can be grouped into tasks for a user in order to have the system perform the heavy lifting. having individual functions may enable users to perform the various functions in different ways allowing an *out-of-band* process of sorts. However, having processes implemented as first-class citizens does add a useful structure to your solution. You may even go with a hybrid approach where some steps require user intervention to continue.

Object State vs. Object Type vs. Object Lifetime

The objects within our broader domain change as time goes by. These changes need to be handled correctly; it may be quite easy to apply the *State Pattern* incorrectly to such a situation. The correct way to use the *State Pattern* is when using the same object but indicating what that object is currently doing. The archetypal sample of this pattern is the vending machine. As actions take place within the machine so the state transitions occur. The vending machine, however, stays a vending machine.

Now how about an egg? Is it a chicken in another state? Let's say we want to track all our eggs. Each is assigned a number. Then one-day egg number 1 "dies". Do we care about the egg? How about the cost of getting the egg to the point it was before it "died"? The next day egg number 2 hatches. Do we care about this egg? It no longer exists. We do care about chicken number 1, though. But after six weeks, chicken number one becomes roast chicken number 20. The chicken is gone.

This is where CQRS can play a role. In our transaction store we could

Hard Edges

start with the two eggs and track all the required information and reporting data in the reporting store. Once egg number 1 dies we can remove it from the transaction store. All the historical data remains in the reporting store. However, the *state* of that egg has probably changed to "dead" though. The same goes for egg number 2. Its state changed to "hatched"; but suddenly we now have a chicken added to our chicken repository. Once the chicken is roasted we can remove the chicken from our checking repository in the transactional store since all the audit data is still in the query store and the chicken is, well, history. But now we have an extra item added to the `RoastedChickenRepository`.

The same idea goes for a `Quote` leading to an `Order` leading to an `Invoice` leading a `PaymentReceivedTransaction`; each living and dying as it transitions along the path. Each entity has a lifecycle in our transaction store. The reporting store never forgets (well, it doesn't *have* to) and is the keeper of all things good and bad that happened.

Code Comments

I am in the camp that proposes no comments. If you need documentation for complex explanations, then that is where the intricacies should be defined.

Hard Edges

```
1   var inputDate = {date we obtained from
        front-end};
2
3   // checks if date is in the future
        (explaining)
4   if (inputDate > DateTime.Now)
5   {
6       throw new ApplicationException("Date
            cannot be in the future.");
7   }
8
9   if (IsFutureDate(inputDate))
10  {
11      throw new ApplicationException("Date
            cannot be in the future.");
12  }
```

The above is perhaps a very simple example but the point is to use the code to *document* the functionality by making it explicit where necessary. The `IsFutureDate()` pretty much tells us what it is going to be doing.

Logging

I have recently been wondering whether one cannot approach logging in a fashion similar to the *no-comment* movement. Instead of logging it may be an option to rather place enough check in the relevant functionality and then throw exceptions for invalid data as opposed to logging.

Our data should be correct. For certain scenarios where we do not necessarily store data we may need to log operations to see what the system is doing but automated unit tests may provide an even better option.

If we *do* need logging then perhaps moving it to a *higher* level, outside of the domain, may be the appropriate place.

What to do vs. How to do it

We are taught that business folks should tell us *what* to do and not *how* to do it. These type of arguments I tend to equate to the following, rather old, riddle:

Three friends go to the same café lunch each day and one day their bill amounts to $30. They each give the waiter $10 but at the till the manager tells the waiter that these people are such good customers that they are going to get a discount of $5. The waiter turns out to be somewhat of a criminal and decides to keep $2 for himself. He goes back to the table and hands each customer $1. Now, if each of the three customers paid $9 that would be 3 * $9 which would be equal to $27. The waiter has $2. $27 + $2 is equal to $29. Where did the other $1 go? The answer lies in the fact that the calculation is approach from different, incorrect, angles. The customers did not pay $27 but $25. The discount was $5 (3 x $1 + $2).

I believe that we need to *not* only know what to do from a business point-of-view but also *how* to do it. They certainly should not be trying to tell us *how* to do it from a *technical* point-of-view. The technical implementation is up to us but if we do not know how to solve the business case on a logical level there is going to be a disconnect between the business concepts and the technical solution. This may be why we run into so many situations where the business folks say that the solution isn't anywhere near what they asked for.

Scalability, Maintainability, Reusability, Reachability

Most *-ilities* can be summed up as "how easy is it *to do*?". These things are typically quite difficult to measure and may, in fact, add to technical debt quite a bit if not considered carefully when architecting your solution. These are broader design issues that do not necessarily affect any of your domain modelling. However, having a domain model eases *all* of these factors.

Most domain models, irrespective of maturity, are going to be quite simple to expose via any integration interface and since you can make use of the domain model from anywhere you are going to be able to scale quite nicely. Security, however, is an application concern that should be outside the domain model.

Complex vs Advanced

Lastly, I'd like to again mention this bit. I have run into many folks that are of the opinion that domain modelling is too complex. A domain model represents business requirements. Never start out looking at domain modelling code. If you understand the business requirements, then the domain model will make sense. Domain modelling may be somewhat more *advanced* than traditional options but it is not in-and-of-itself complex. Once understood and with sufficient experience quite the contrary may be true.

Epilogue

Thank you for taking the time to read this guidance. If you have any comments or suggestions, please contact me@ebenroux.co.za and let me know. Since it is an e-book I can keep updating and republishing to make it more useful to the Domain-Driven Design community.

Printed in Poland
by Amazon Fulfillment
Poland Sp. z o.o., Wrocław